RICH PEOPLE
POOR COUNTRIES

The Rise of
Emerging-Market Tycoons
and their Mega Firms

Caroline Freund

Assisted by Sarah Oliver

FSC
www.fsc.org

MIX
Paper from
responsible sources
FSC® C005010

RICH PEOPLE
POOR COUNTRIES

The Rise of Emerging-Market Tycoons and their Mega Firms

Caroline Freund

Assisted by Sarah Oliver

Peterson Institute for International Economics

Washington, DC

January 2016

Caroline Freund is senior fellow at the Peterson Institute for International Economics. Prior to joining the Institute, she was chief economist for the Middle East and North Africa at the World Bank. She has also worked in the research departments of the World Bank, the International Monetary Fund, and the Federal Reserve Board. She has published numerous articles in economics journals and has contributed to many edited volumes. Her work has been cited in leading magazines and newspapers, including *Business Week*, *Economist*, *Financial Times*, *New York Times*, *Wall Street Journal*, and *Washington Post*. She is a member of the US Export-Import Bank Advisory Committee and teaches trade policy at Johns Hopkins School of Advanced International Studies. She is on the scientific committees of CEPII (Institute for Research of the International Economy, Paris) and the Economic Research Forum (Cairo) and is a member of the Center for Economic Policy Research.

PETERSON INSTITUTE FOR INTERNATIONAL ECONOMICS
1750 Massachusetts Avenue, NW
Washington, DC 20036-1903
(202) 328-9000   FAX: (202) 328-5432
www.piie.com

Adam S. Posen, *President*
Steven R. Weisman, *Vice President for Publications and Communications*

Cover Design by Peggy Archambault
Cover Photos: iStock ©Evgeny Sergeev, iStock ©rasslava
Printed by Versa Press, Inc.

Printed in the United States of America
18   17   16   5   4   3   2   1

Library of Congress Cataloging-in-Publication Data
Freund, Caroline L.
  Rich people poor countries: the rise of emerging-market tycoons and their mega firms/Caroline Freund; assisted by Sarah Oliver.
    pages cm
  Includes bibliographical references.
  ISBN 978-0-88132-703-8
  1. Developing countries—Economic conditions. 2. Nouveau riche—Developing countries. 3. Entrepreneurship—Developing countries. 4. Equality—Developing countries. 5. Income distribution—Developing countries. I. Title.
  HC59.7.F696 2015
  338.9009172′4—dc23

                                    2015017553

This publication has been subjected to a prepublication peer review intended to ensure analytical quality. The views expressed are those of the author. This publication is part of the overall program of the Peterson Institute for International Economics, as endorsed by its Board of Directors, but it does not necessarily reflect the views of individual members of the Board or of the Institute's staff or management.
The Peterson Institute for International Economics is a private nonpartisan, nonprofit institution for rigorous, intellectually open, and indepth study and discussion of international economic policy. Its purpose is to identify and analyze important issues to make globalization beneficial and sustainable for the people of the United States and the world, and then to develop and communicate practical new approaches for dealing with them.
Its work is funded by a highly diverse group of philanthropic foundations, private corporations, and interested individuals, as well as income on its capital fund. About 35 percent of the Institute's resources in its latest fiscal year were provided by contributors from outside the United States. A list of all financial supporters for the preceding four years is posted at http://piie.com/supporters.cfm.

Contents

Tables

Figures

Map

Preface

Policymakers, academics, and the media increasingly view the rising wealth of the top 0.00001 percent of individuals as a problem irrespective of how wealth is accrued. The statistics on the growing number of billionaires in the world and their share of global wealth are indeed stunning: Billionaire wealth has grown over 500 percent in the last 18 years (1996–2014), while global income has risen only by 148 percent. This raises concerns about a future where the superrich get richer while the poor and middle classes see their wealth (if any) stagnate.

Caroline Freund reminds us that extreme wealth is also in many cases a reward for major innovation, and as a result the growth in extreme wealth can be a sign that things are going very well, depending on who exactly is getting rich. She examines how the richest men and women in the world made their fortunes to understand whether the new superrich are rising innovators or whether their wealth stems from bequests or political connections.

The results are striking. Extreme wealth in emerging markets is growing more rapidly than in advanced countries but unlike advanced countries, where the relative shares of inheritors and self-made billionaires are fairly flat, extreme wealth in emerging markets is dominated by self-made men (and a handful of women). Importantly, within this group of the self-made rich in emerging markets, the fastest growing group is that of the innovators, people building large companies that are intricately linked with global markets. The large-scale entrepreneurs and their businesses are helping to modernize these economies by pulling workers out of rural agriculture and into the urban workforce. In contrast, the advanced countries appear more stagnant in their sources of wealth accumulation, and this parallels growth developments, with the Anglo countries in particular revealing some worrying trends.

Freund presents compelling evidence that the presence of these large global firms founded by innovators is important for everyone's economic growth and modernization. She brings together a wealth of recent empirical evidence using firm-level data that show case after case that resource allocation between specific business firms matters for growth. Productivity growth is the result not just of better technologies but also to a great extent of improved resource allocation between firms. Richer countries have a larger share of their workforce in large firms, economic growth is associated with an expansion of large firms, and exports come almost entirely from the largest firms in a country. When the most productive firms employ more capital and labor output expands, there are more jobs, and those jobs pay higher wages.

The important role played by large firms in spurring economic growth goes against the commonly held view that small and medium-sized enterprises are the key to innovation and must be supported by government policies. Similarly, her findings suggest that concerns about the "missing middle" in the firm size distribution in developing countries are unfounded. In fact, what developing economies need are export-superstar large firms. The argument made in this book is that productivity growth requires that resources flow seamlessly to the most productive firms allowing these firms to grow large. This does not mean that governments should favor large firms—ease of firm entry is important, so new firms can enter and grow rapidly if they are competitive—just that there must not be constraints limiting the growth of the most productive firms. Openness to trade is also critical because it guides resources to their most productive uses and offers a market large enough for competitive firms to grow into. An improved business climate and openness to trade have facilitated the rise of big business (and its accompanying group of wealthy entrepreneurs) in all of the successful industrializations of the past and is seen in the growth success stories (and emerging-market billionaires) of today. Freund's exciting empirical analysis derived from corporate performance today evokes comparisons to economic development of the US Gilded Age of the late 19th century, suggesting that emerging economies need tycoons in order to rise.

The Peterson Institute for International Economics is a private nonpartisan, nonprofit institution for rigorous, intellectually open, and indepth study and discussion of international economic policy. Its purpose is to identify and analyze important issues to making globalization beneficial and sustainable for the people of the United States and the world, and then to develop and communicate practical new approaches for dealing with them.

The Institute's work is funded by a highly diverse group of philanthropic foundations, private corporations, and interested individuals, as well as by income on its capital fund. About 35 percent of the Institute's resources in our latest fiscal year were provided by contributors from outside the United States. This book is part of the Institute's project on Inequality and Inclusive Capitalism, which is partially supported by a series of major grants from the ERANDA Foundation. A list of all our financial supporters for the preceding year is posted at http://www.piie.com/supporters.cfm.

The Executive Committee of the Institute's Board of Directors bears overall responsibility for the Institute's direction, gives general guidance and approval to its research program, and evaluates its performance in pursuit of its mission. The Institute's President is responsible for the identification of topics that are likely to become important over the medium term (one to three years) that should be addressed by Institute scholars. This rolling agenda is set in close consultation with the Institute's research staff, Board of Directors, and other stakeholders.

The President makes the final decision to publish any individual Institute study, following independent internal and external review of the work. Interested readers may access the data and computations underlying Institute publications for research and replication by searching titles at www.piie.com.

The Institute hopes that its research and other activities will contribute to building a stronger foundation for international economic policy around the world. We invite readers of these publications to let us know how they think we can best accomplish this objective.

Adam S. Posen
President
November 2015

Acknowledgments

This book would not exist without support from Sarah Oliver. She helped create and analyze the many datasets used in this book and kept all of the data and files documented and well organized. Without implicating any of them, there are many people I would like to thank for help in finishing this book. In the early stages of writing I benefited tremendously from a presentation to PIIE senior fellows, as well as written comments from Bill Cline, Tomáš Hellebrandt, Gary Hufbauer, Simon Johnson, Nick Lardy, Paolo Mauro, Marcus Noland, Robert Lawrence, Arvind Subramanian, Ted Truman, Steve Weisman, and Nicolas Véron. I also benefited from a study group held at PIIE to discuss the manuscript and especially comments from Rabah Azrezki, Shanta Devarajan, Simeon Djankov, and Martha Denisse Pierola. I am especially grateful to Branko Milanović for detailed comments, suggestions, and discussions, which helped shape this book.

I am also extremely grateful to three formal peer reviewers, Surjit Bhalla, Chang-Tai Hsieh, and Aaditya Mattoo, all of whom made very constructive comments that reshaped the manuscript further; they also pushed me to take the data further in some places and to be more precise in others. Participants at a number of presentations provided useful comments, including at the International Monetary Fund, the World Bank, PIIE's Board of Directors' meeting, CF40-PIIE conference in Beijing, an invited lecture for the business community in Shanghai, and the Moody's annual conference in Dubai.

I would also like to thank PIIE president Adam Posen for his strong support and for providing me with valuable guidance throughout. I am also grateful to Steve Weisman for helping with production and overseeing the publications team including Barbara Karni, Madona Devasahayam, and Susann Luetjen, all of whom provided excellent editorial and publishing assistance on the manuscript.

Finally, I am very grateful to Sir Evelyn de Rothschild and Lynn Forester de Rothschild for generously supporting this project through a grant to the Institute for work on inequality and inclusive capitalism.

Overview

In 1999 an English teacher in Hangzhou, China, started a company in his apartment connecting small Chinese exporters to potential customers abroad. The teacher was Jack Ma. His company, Alibaba, has made him the richest man in China today. Starting with 18 friends and students, Ma has built his company into one that employs 24,000 people and moves more goods than Amazon and eBay combined. In September 2014, Alibaba issued the largest global initial public offering in history, when its market value surpassed that of Facebook. Alibaba's market capitalization overtook that of Walmart and GE a few months later. Jack Ma is worth an estimated $21 billion.

After working in the pharmaceutical distribution business, Dilip Shanghvi borrowed 10,000 rupees (about $1,000 in the 1980s) from his father to start a drug company. His company, established in 1983, produced lithium, a medication to treat bipolar disorder. The company made its first sales in 1987 and started exporting in 1989 and carrying out research in 1991. Sun Pharma went public in 1994. In 2014 it was worth $27 billion, making Shanghvi (worth $12.8 billion) the second-richest man in India. Sun Pharma is the largest drug company in India, employing 16,000 people.

In 1959 Ahmet Nazif Zorlu dropped out of high school at age 15 to work in his family's small textile business in Babadag, Turkey, a mountain village the size of Luray, Virginia. By the mid-1970s, Zorlu was the boss. He embraced technology, logistics, and global markets, transforming the company into a mega-factory producing curtains and polyester yarn. By the 1990s the company dominated world markets in these products. It expanded into other industries, applying the same modern production and distribution techniques Zorlu had brought to textiles. One of the most notable acquisitions was Vestel, a bankrupt television manufacturer. By 2000 the revamped company had captured one-quarter of the European television market and was a major exporter of washing machines and refrigerators. The Zorlu Group employs 30,000 people and accounts for more than 3 percent of Turkey's total manufacturing exports. Ahmet Nazif Zorlu is worth $2 billion.

These three success stories tell a story that is strikingly at odds with conventional wisdom about the rise of wealth in recent years in developing countries. The examples demonstrate that prosperity is not necessarily a result of crony capitalism, unfair business advantages or control of natural resources, monopolies, and favoritism. In fact, a new billionaire class has emerged that is testimony to innovation, creativity, ingenuity, and other capitalist skills traditionally associated with advanced economies. Far from disadvantaging poor and middle-class workers, these billionaires have compiled an impressive record of providing employment opportunities that have raised living standards and increased economic stability in countries that have not always enjoyed success in these areas.

The examples of Ma, Shanghvi, and Zorlu tell only the beginning of the story. In China the leaders of globally ranked companies like Huawei, Lenovo, Alibaba, Xiaomi, ZTE, Hisense, and Tencent are all worth hundreds of millions of dollars or more. Knowledge- and technology-intensive industries now account for 20 percent of China's GDP, four-fifths of which comes from private firms. Shanghvi is one of a number of pharmaceutical leaders in India: Dr. Reddy's Laboratories Ltd., Cipla, Lupin, Aurobindo, Cadila, Jubilant, Ipca, Torrent, and Wockhardt are among India's largest companies. All have annual sales of more than $1 billion, and most have manufacturing plants outside of India; many of their founders are billionaires. India is now the third-largest pharmaceutical producer in the world.

Thanks to Zorlu and other appliance producers, Turkey has become known throughout Europe for high-quality, low-price durable goods. Along with Vestel, the Turkish giant Arcelik is home to the Beko brand and part of Koç Holding, which accounts for 8 percent of Turkey's GDP and 10 percent of the country's exports. It is the only Turkish company in the Fortune 500. The Koç family is among the wealthiest in Turkey.

Entrepreneurs who build large companies are becoming increasingly common in emerging markets.[1] Before the growth spurt of the 2000s, the

---

1. For expositional purposes, the terms *developing country*, *emerging market*, and *South* are used interchangeably to refer to countries outside the high-income OECD. The terms *advanced* or *developed countries* and *North* refer to high-income OECD countries.

vast majority of the superrich outside advanced countries inherited their wealth, made it from resources, or reaped unearned benefits accrued not from productive investment but from government connections, government-sanctioned monopolies, or privatizations that benefited people with connections. This group of so-called rent seekers or rentiers got rich not from supreme talent or innovation but because of commodity price movements and/or government connections.

Today an expanding group of successful emerging-market entrepreneurs building large companies is getting extraordinarily wealthy. Many are transforming global markets as their companies compete for customers and investment opportunities around the world. In 2004 just 20 percent of the 587 billionaires identified by Forbes in its World's Billionaires List were from emerging markets. A decade later 43 percent of the world's 1,645 billionaires were from emerging markets. More than 500 emerging-market fortunes were added over this period, and founders of non-resource-based, nonfinance companies contributed more to that growth than any other group.

These gains are reflected in the lists of the largest companies, which show a similar trend. Emerging-market firms made up 30 percent of the 2014 Fortune 500 list, more than twice their share a decade earlier. Forbes Global 2000, a list of the world's 2,000 largest companies, shows the same expansion. Given current trends, by 2025, 45 percent of Fortune 500 companies and 50 percent of the world's billionaires are expected to come from emerging markets.

These business leaders are helping drive emerging-market growth. Because an increasing share of the new money is earned from innovative companies, as opposed to rents and inheritance, it is associated with job creation and growth. The effects are extending beyond local markets. Many entrepreneurs are gearing their products to foreign markets, building subsidiaries around the world, and enhancing global competition. Although a sizable share of wealth still accrues to owners of property and resources (inducing distributional rather than productive consequences), large-scale entrepreneurship is growing rapidly in the developing world.

Tycoonomics: Big Firms, Big Money, and Development

This book argues that the creation of large corporations and the accompanying rise in extreme wealth are inevitably part of the development process. The record suggests in case after case that as countries develop, a handful of exceptionally productive firms grow rapidly and become giants, making the founders spectacularly wealthy. Even when foreign investment catalyzes the process, the economic transformation happens when large-scale domestic entrepreneurship follows. The new company leaders are not satisfied with dominating local markets. Their mega firms are increasingly targeting global markets. Many operate production facilities around the world, and some are buying and restructuring well-established firms in advanced countries.

Successful companies are not just a product of the development process. They add to that process. One way that company founders in emerging markets contribute to development is to provide more and better jobs through the firms that they create. They accelerate the normal development process in agrarian-based poor economies by pulling resources out of subsistence agriculture and into industry and services, expanding the middle class. It is not a coincidence that all countries that have developed rapidly over the past 200 years have experienced some version of this process of "tycoonomics."

In principle, extreme wealth is not a necessary ingredient for development to occur. The majority of firms in an economy could grow relatively rapidly, yielding modest wealth for many, without extreme wealth. But this does not happen in practice. Alternatively, state-owned firms could drive industrialization, but such firms have been incapable of producing sustainable growth. Achieving more than a decade of strong growth requires vibrant private sector, where new firms drive out weak firms and the strongest firms grow very large. In fact, a growing body of evidence shows that a relatively small number of privately owned superstar firms with stellar growth supports rapid economic growth better than either broad-based growth across most firms in an economy or the rise of state-owned firms. The smartest, pushiest, and luckiest of the founders of this group of firms become the superrich.

The importance of a few large firms in driving growth is an illustration of the first principle of economics: that when resources are scarce, the allocation of capital and labor is critical to a country's potential output. Until recently, economists thought that only the allocation of capital and labor across industries was important. If capital and labor flowed to the sectors where they were used most productively, a country would grow rapidly. Recent research, using newly available firm-level data, shows that some firms are many times more productive than others, even within the same sector. As a result, not only is growth stronger when capital and labor flow to the sectors where they are most productive but also the resources must move to the most productive firms in those sectors. For example, if capital is more productive in the cloth sector than the food sector, raising incomes is not just about pulling capital out of food and into cloth but also about pulling resources to the most productive firms in the cloth sector. Accordingly, growth in a small number of superstar firms that use capital and labor most efficiently is an important factor in economic development.

Structure of the Book

This book is divided into four parts. Part I develops a system of classification, or taxonomy, of the superrich and their sources of wealth, splitting them into five categories:

1. people who inherit wealth,
2. company founders,
3. company executives,
4. government-connected billionaires whose wealth derives from natural resources, privatizations, or other connections to the government, i.e., rent-related billionaires, and
5. finance and real estate billionaires.

The most surprising conclusion resulting from this taxonomy is the significant shift between 2001 and 2014 to company founders and executives in emerging markets (and the slight decline in this group's share in advanced countries). Among the superrich in emerging markets, company leaders are twice as prevalent as they were in 2001. This shift took place despite soaring commodity prices, which pulled capital and labor into those rent-related sectors in many emerging-market countries. The shift, moreover, is absent in advanced countries, despite the rise of new technology giants. This part of the book examines the sectors and countries that are a main force behind the change. It highlights East Asia, the most dynamic region, and the Middle East and North Africa, the only emerging-market region in which the share of inherited wealth expanded and the share of company founders declined.

Part II attributes the expansion of wealth to the role of large firms, and even individual firms, in economic growth. Three important trends are occurring in many emerging markets: the rise of mega firms, the emergence of extreme wealth, and rapid income growth. The evidence suggests that the three trends are closely related. Recent research shows that when economies perform well, the most productive firms grow rapidly. Development requires reallocating resources to highly productive firms and allowing them to mature into mega firms. The development of the mega firms helps to transform a country's economic structure as these firms pull workers out of agriculture and into industry. The firms tend to be in internationally competitive industries and thrive because they are among the best in the world at what they do and are competitive on global markets. As these firms attract more resources, the wealth of their founders grows.

The emergence of mega firms in the fastest-growing emerging markets is similar to the growth of big business during the rapid modernizations of the United States and Europe in the late 19th and early 20th centuries, Japan after World War II, and Korea in the 1960s and 1970s. The economic historian Alfred Chandler (1992) has demonstrated the crucial role of big business in creating economic growth during these episodes. Much of what he has written applies to the more recent modernizers. For example, mechanization of food packaging allowed family-owned companies like Heinz and Campbell Soup to thrive in the United States, just as innovation has allowed Tee Yih Jia Foods (the world leader in spring roll pastry) to thrive in Asia and M. Dias Branco (a leading manufacturer and distributor of pasta, cookies, and other goods) in Latin America. The chemicals industry in Germany developed because BASF, Bayer, and Hoechst exploited returns to scale. The Indian chemicals industry is now charting a similar path. The role Chandler envisions for big business in economic development is as visible in the emerging markets now as it was in advanced countries, with the fastest-growing countries recording an increasing share of the world's largest companies.

The relationship proposed here between extreme wealth and development follows from the association between big business and development, such that they all move together. The evidence indicates, moreover, that extreme wealth not only is associated with development but also in fact contributes to it. Figure O.1 shows a scatter plot of the number of billionaires per million and GDP per capita. The two are tightly linked, especially during the period of structural transformation, when economies move out of agriculture and into industry. Over the past 15 years, for example, China's per capita income rose from less than $3,000 to more than $10,000 (in 2011 purchasing power parity international dollars); the steep slope indicates that the wealthy population grows especially rapidly during this stage. When countries are very rich, the relationship is flatter. Part II of the book presents evidence that a higher density of extremely wealthy people is associated with structural transformation in emerging markets but not in advanced countries. Controlling for the level of development, more billionaires per capita is associated with more employment in industry and less in agriculture. The section also shows that trade is more important for emerging-market companies and their owners than it is for advanced-country firms and their owners.

Figure O.1   Correlation between density of billionaires and stage of economic development

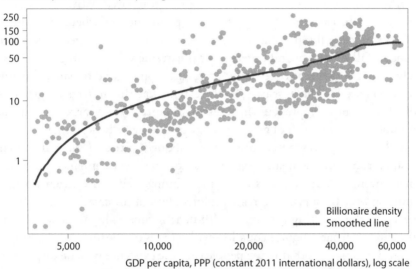

billionaires per 100 million people, log scale

GDP per capita, PPP (constant 2011 international dollars), log scale

PPP = purchasing power parity

Sources: Data from Forbes, The World's Billionaires; and World Bank, *World Development Indicators.*

The evidence on wealth, big business, and structural transformation is consistent with the emergence of extreme wealth as part of the development process. To the extent that the best entrepreneurs in emerging markets create globally competitive firms and attract labor and capital, they are steering resources to more productive uses. The resulting increase in productivity helps countries to grow and develop. The development is broad-based because the mega firms create jobs, improving the lives of the poor and middle classes, and these jobs pay relatively high wages. In this way, the route to extreme wealth is an integral part of the modernization process because wealth and modernization both rely on the creation of big business. The existence of extreme wealth owing to innovation can be especially beneficial in emerging markets, because entrepreneurs are likely to be better intermediaries of capital than governments, and the lack of deep financial markets means that the concentration of wealth may make the large investments needed for industrialization feasible.

If the new emerging-market superrich are creating the big businesses for development, exploring their characteristics will provide insight into how business may grow and change over time. Part III explores the age and gender of billionaires, the age of their firms, and the extent of turnover.

Emerging-market billionaires tend to be younger than advanced-country billionaires, looking more like the new technology billionaires. Their companies are also relatively young: The median firm of a self-made billionaire in the South was just 28 years old in 2014, compared with 47 years old in the North. There is a strong up-or-out phenomenon, where individuals who cross the billion-dollar threshold either continue to get richer over time or fall off the list all together—it is extremely rare to stagnate. As in advanced countries, very few billionaires are women, and female company founders are especially scarce. To the extent that this reflects bigger hurdles for female entrepreneurs in accessing finance to grow large companies, it implies that a wealth of great ideas are not being fully exploited.

Part IV explores potential concerns about the rise in inequality that results from extreme wealth, even when extreme wealth enhances development overall. Policy options to promote innovation and efficiency while limiting wealth concentration are explored. Even if the creation of big business and the resulting extreme wealth benefit those who are less well off, the current debate about inequality—with a focus on the top of the distribution—demonstrates that many people find the existence of wide disparities in wealth and income to be morally unacceptable and dangerous to political stability. As an Oxfam report (Seery and Arendar 2014) notes, it is hard for many people to stomach the fact that a single double-decker bus of people has more wealth than the bottom half of the global population. As the billionaire bus fills with people speaking Chinese, Hindi, and other non-European languages, these concerns may be magnified, because the compatriots of the newly arrived billionaires are relatively poor: The gap in living standards between Jack Ma and the average Chinese worker is greater than the gap between Bill Gates and the average American worker.

But the disparity of incomes is not the only measure that matters when thinking about equity. Improvements in living standards of rich and poor alike may be an equally or even more important metric for evaluating the impact of the rise of the very rich. By this metric, inequality in poor countries appears to be a very different phenomenon from inequality in advanced countries. In the advanced countries of the so-called North, billionaire-level wealth grew three times as fast as aggregate incomes between 2006 and 2014. By contrast, aggregate incomes grew faster than the incomes of those in the extreme wealthy class in the poor countries of the South. To put it another way, Jack Ma's compatriots have seen their incomes grow alongside his own; Bill Gates' have not. This phenomenon may explain why it is in the rich countries that people are calling for more equitable distribution while populations in the South remain more concerned about economic growth and jobs.

Reducing poverty and increasing opportunity—not the rise of the top 1 percent and the stagnation of the rest—remain the most important considerations in emerging markets. The concern about inequality has been raised politically in the wake of the global financial and economic crisis that began in 2007–08, which hit low-income families the hardest and spurred protests over economic fairness on both the left and the right. But the focus on extreme wealth and income inequality among many policymakers and pundits appears to reflect an Anglo bias, as it is largely in the English-speaking world that these trends are especially pronounced. Despite data showing that the rise of the top 1 (or .0001) percent relative to the rest is mainly an Anglo country problem, concerns about extreme incomes and wealth expressed by international institutions tend to treat the problem as a global one.

Economic policymakers in many emerging markets, on the other hand, are less concerned with inequality than with innovation and growth. This requires establishing strong property rights, ease of business entry and exit, and openness to trade and foreign investment. This combination of policies steers resources to their most productive uses while offering the high returns that are necessary to promote large-scale entrepreneurship. Ease of entry and openness to trade ensure that extreme wealth is accruing largely to people competing in contestable industries, not to domestic monopolies.

Even with such policies, however, distortions can prevent large-scale enterprise from developing. To spur large-scale entrepreneurship, concessional financing has proven useful in a number of contexts. It is more successful when it targets the most productive and externally oriented firms than when it supports all firms in a given sector through a broader industrial policy.

As countries develop, the challenge is to avoid creating excessive amounts of unproductive wealth. Estate tax can prevent wealth from accruing on the basis of inheritance as opposed to talent. Part IV discusses policies to limit wealth in sectors that may offer high returns but are relatively unproductive from a social perspective (the clearest example in this category is much of the recent hedge fund wealth).

The rise of an innovative wealthy class in emerging markets is a positive contributor to economic growth and higher living standards. It is not clear, however, how the power associated with wealth will affect political systems. Two issues are particularly important. First, once a new business becomes well established and highly profitable, owners have incentives to erect barriers to entry to protect their market and maintain profits. Strong government ties increase the threat that the wealthy distort government regulation and taxation (what is sometimes called crony capitalism). Second, the power associated with wealth may give the rich disproportionate power over the political system, which can move it away from the interests of the majority. In more authoritarian regimes, where the government does not serve the majority, private wealth may be used to support a regime in exchange for friendly treatment of the associated business. But wealth can also be a force for change, by promoting democracy (as Mikhail Khodorkovsky of Russia and Wang Gongquan of China have tried to do) or demanding institutions that protect property rights (as Daron Acemoglu, Simon Johnson, and James Robinson [2005] show is possible). These issues are not the focus of this book (much has already been written about them) but are discussed briefly in chapters 2 and 5.[2]

A Note on the Approach

The contribution of this book is twofold: It provides a taxonomy of the superrich using the World's Billionaires List from Forbes, and it connects the appearance of large firms and the ensuing wealth to development. Where data permit, the book examines large firms broadly and various levels of wealth, but the focus is on billionaires and their firms, especially the most innovative, whose multinational corporations are transforming economies. The focus is on billionaires not because they are more important for the economy than other big businesspeople but because their main sources of wealth can be traced and the firms they create are highly visible.

The disadvantage of this approach is that it focuses on a very exclusive group; as a result, it does not yield a complete picture of a country's businesses, especially in countries with only one or two billionaires. Even so, a discussion of the characteristics of billionaires can shed light on important issues, such as the role of large businesses and how wealth is created and acquired more generally. The sectoral composition, age, and method of wealth accumulation provide an image, however incomplete, of business and entrepreneurship in that country.

The book examines the appearance of the superrich in emerging markets from a purely economic standpoint. The broad message is that the rise of extreme wealth in emerging markets reflects a new breed of entre-

---

2. A discussion of campaign finance, lobbying, and the rich in office is beyond the scope of this analysis. Darrell West (2014) provides a comprehensive account of the role of wealth in politics in the 21st century, with a focus on the United States. John Kampfner (2014) discusses the controversial relationship between wealth and politics over the past 2,000 years.

preneurs who think beyond local markets and embrace technology and innovation.

The linkage between the creation of large companies and large fortunes is not surprising. Private firms that grow rapidly generate huge fortunes for their founders. Bill Gates is superrich because Microsoft is enormous; Jack Ma is superrich because Alibaba is huge.

What is perhaps more surprising is the tight link between growth in the share of the world's billionaires and growth in the share of the world's Fortune 500 companies from emerging markets. This positive correlation is a sign that the new emerging-market billionaires are not purely agents of political rent seeking, as is commonly thought, but are building mega firms that produce globally recognized brands. These capitalists and their mega firms are related to the extraordinary growth occurring outside advanced countries. They are harnessing the resources of their countries and taking advantage of global markets. That said, there is substantial variation across countries in the importance of innovation and entrepreneurship. And although rent-seeking activities are declining, they still account for about one-fifth of emerging-market fortunes.

I

THE TYCOONS

1

Who Are the Superrich?

A World Economic Forum panel in January 2015 discussed the rise of the superrich. Winnie Byanyima, the executive director of Oxfam, began the conversation with the observation that in 2014, 85 people had as much wealth as the bottom 50 percent of the world's population and that in 2015, 80 would have as much. She expressed concern about such extreme inequality as a worrisome trend, irrespective of how worthy were the means by which the wealthy achieved their success.[1] Sir Martin Sorrell, CEO of WPP, a large marketing firm, retorted, "I make no apology for having started a company 30 years ago with 2 people and having 179,000 people in 111 countries and investing in human capital each year to the tune of at least \$12 billion a year."[2] His comment showed that it was wrong to label all wealth as inherently worrisome because in his case it resulted from an enterprising initiative that benefited many others.

Is the increase in extreme wealth around the world a worrisome trend, regardless of how it was gained or invested, as Byanyima fears, or a source of economic growth, as Sorrell proposes? Is it indicative of less legitimate methods, such as state capture, favoritism, unfair advantage (inheritance or access to resources or monopolies)? Or is it a reflection of the value of prosperity, as new businesses flourish and create jobs? This chapter identifies different types of wealth by presenting a taxonomy that attempts to separate "company creators" from other members of the superrich class

---

1. "Davos: A Richer World—But for Whom?" BBC, January 23, 2015.

2. Ibid.

and understand how this group has changed over time. Its argument is that the growing importance of independent company creation has brought wide benefits in poor and emerging economies and that these gains must be evaluated in a broader context than simply a judgment of whether inequality itself is bad for a country.

Self-made billionaires represent a growing share of the world's billionaire population. But much of their wealth comes from finance and politically connected/rent-related activities. For the world as a whole, the share of billionaires who founded companies has been roughly flat at nearly 30 percent.

These global trends, however, obscure significant variation between advanced countries and emerging markets. Emerging-market billionaires are more likely to be self-made and their wealth tied to government-related activities. The share of billionaires who are company founders in emerging markets is on the rise, while inheritors are in decline. In contrast, in advanced countries, wealth shares are relatively stagnant, with a modest decline in inherited wealth and company founders and an increase in finance-, rent-, and government-related wealth.

This chapter presents theories about why extreme wealth has grown. It identifies five types of billionaires: people who inherit wealth, company founders, executives, government-connected or rent-related billionaires, and finance and real estate billionaires.

How and Why Do People Become Very Rich?

Economic thinking offers three broad explanations for the extraordinary rise of top incomes and wealth in recent decades.

Superstardom

The first theory, associated with Alfred Marshall (1890) and more recently Sherwin Rosen (1981), puts exceptional ability, technological change, and globalization at the heart of extreme incomes and hence wealth. According to this view, growth in extreme wealth stems from changes in the environment that have made today the right time and place for superstars to create and grow truly innovative enterprises. The "superstar" theory argues that new technologies allow people to communicate more easily, enhancing returns to scale, while globalization provides a nearly unlimited audience. With new communications technology, a superstar manager can now manage people around the world, just as a superstar singer could be heard globally following the advent of recording devices. Lower barriers to trade and investment and cross-continental travel yield access to a wider customer base and allow for more efficient production techniques. Just as Hollywood stars attract wide audiences and large salaries, while starving actors abound, company leaders now reap enormous rewards while middle management stagnates. As a result, superstars in many fields, especially new technologies, are in high demand and earn extraordinary wages while demand for the skills of most people remains stagnant or worse.

Technology has rewarded many superstars, such as Mark Zuckerberg, the founder of Facebook (number 21 on the 2014 Forbes World's Billionaires List), and Azim Premji (number 61), the founder of India's third-largest software outsourcing firm, Wipro. But techies are not the only billionaire entrepreneurs: Trade and technology have also rewarded goods producers. Amancio Ortega, the founder of the international clothing retailer Zara, is the world's third-richest person. More than 70 percent of his stores are outside his home country of Spain. Trade is also important for He Xiangjian of China (190th on the Forbes list), whose fortunes stem from the appliance producer Midea, which earns about half of its revenues from exports.

Extraction of Rent

The superstar theory presumes entrepreneurship on the part of the rich. But not all wealth is acquired in virtuous ways. Extraction of rent is the second broad explanation proposed for the rise in extreme wealth. It is potentially more important in emerging markets, where institutions are less developed. This argument emphasizes government interventions, such as privatization and regulation, soaring asset prices, and changes in corporate culture and social norms, all of which allow a larger share of rents to accrue to a small group of capital owners without a corresponding rise in the real productivity of capital or its owners. Unlike the wealth created by superstars, this type of extreme wealth does not improve allocative efficiency.

Examples of rent extraction include much of the oil wealth in emerging markets as well as a number of underpriced privatizations. Nigeria's Foloronsho Alakija (number 687 on the Forbes list) benefited from a cheap oil license granted by the government. Her wealth expanded dramatically as oil prices surged in recent years, bringing her to the Forbes list for the first time in 2014. Russia's Igor Makarov (number 828), who first appeared on the list in 2012, became a billionaire following a joint venture with Rostneft, the Russian state oil company.

Not all rent-related wealth comes from natural resources. Brazil's Cesar Mata Pires (number 1,143), founder of construction company OAS, appeared on the list for the first time after winning the government contract (and subsidized government loans) to build Brazil's 2014 World Cup stadiums.

Inheritance

The third source of expanding wealth is inheritance, which leads to a consolidation of wealth if returns to wealth exceed growth and capital grows rapidly. Thomas Piketty argues that because historically capital earns higher returns than labor, the rich will continue to get richer unless global tax policies change. Inheritance plays an important role in this theory, because capital's share of income grows faster than labor's share. For this phenomenon to increase inequality over the long run, it must be the case that capital is not easily created or destroyed. France's Liliane Bettencourt, one of the richest women in the world, is a prime example of the growth of inherited wealth. In 2000 her estimated net worth was $15 billion; by 2014 it had more than doubled to $38 billion. This fortune accumulated as a result of her large stakes in L'Oréal and Nestlé.

However, large inheritances do not always grow, as the relatively high return on capital that Piketty worries about is an aggregate measure and reflects returns to many different investments both old and new. Carlos Peralta, for example, inherited a manufacturing and construction conglomerate from his father. He expanded into telecoms with the help of a cell phone license awarded by the government, putting him on the Forbes list from 1999 to 2004. His fortune reversed in 2005 as the Mexican economy became more competitive, taking him off the list. In 2009 the global recession hit his businesses hard, forcing him to put his 257-foot yacht and Trump Tower apartment on the market.

Because of new wealth creation and the fact that a good deal of old wealth is destroyed, inherited wealth has not been growing as a share of total wealth in either the North or the South.

Determinants of Extreme Wealth

Empirical research on the rise of the superrich—most of which focuses on the developed world—is inconclusive. Some evidence suggests that technology and globalization are the sources of extreme wealth. Other research finds that the rise in asset prices and changes in corporate governance are key.[3]

---

3. Facundo Alvaredo et al. (2013a) argue that there is a wide variety of outcomes in advanced countries—with some countries but not others showing a sharp increase in income at the top—indicating that forces common to all industrial countries, such as new technology and globalization, cannot be responsible for the rising share of the top 1 percent. Thomas Piketty and Emmanuel Saez (2013) echo this view, noting the strong correlation between the income of the top percentile and reductions in top tax rates. Using detailed US income tax data for 1979-2005, Jon Bakija, Adam Cole, and Bradly Heim (2012) find stark differences in pay differentials across occupations. They show that executives, managers, supervisors, and

Little academic research has explored the phenomenal rise in extreme wealth in emerging markets. But private banks and consulting firms have jumped in to tap this growing market. The Boston Consulting Company has written extensively about the superrich in Asia, as both a byproduct of and a foundation for growth. Banks in Europe struggling with new regulations are "fighting over rich emerging-market clients to boost revenue."[4] Ruchir Sharma, of Morgan Stanley, has been tracking how billionaires in emerging markets made their fortunes to glean "a quick indicator of how well positioned emerging nations are to compete in the global economy."[5] With a similar goal in mind, the taxonomy presented in this chapter expands on the Forbes data to develop a methodology for comparing the sources of wealth across countries.

The 2014 Forbes World's Billionaires List includes 1,645 individuals from 69 countries, 959 of them from advanced countries and 686 from emerging markets. The rise in extreme wealth in emerging markets over the past 10 to 15 years has been dramatic, with 42 percent of billionaires coming from emerging markets in 2014. The Forbes list is the longest series of data and includes the names of individual billionaires, facilitating research into the origins of wealth. Other data sources show similar patterns for the years for which they have data. Knight Frank and Wealth-X both put the emerging-market share at 43 percent. They also provide information on individuals worth tens or hundreds of millions of dollars. These data are useful to expand country coverage, as smaller countries often have no billionaires. Knight Frank (2014) finds that 25 percent of people worth $100 million and 22 percent of people worth $10 million or more are from emerging markets. These shares are about twice what they were a decade ago. Wealth-X and UBS (2014) estimate that 28 percent of the ultra-high-net-worth population (people worth $30 million or more) live in emerging markets.

This section compares the 2001 Forbes list to the 2014 list in order to better understand the composition of today's billionaires. The 2001 Forbes list provided no information about the source of billionaire wealth. More recent lists include the company or industry associated with each

---

financial professionals account for about 60 percent of the top 0.1 percent in recent years and argue that asset prices and possibly corporate governance are the primary sources of the increase in extreme wealth. Steven Kaplan and Joshua Rauh (2013) examine both income and wealth in the United States and find in favor of technology, largely because change is spread broadly across occupations.

4. "BNP Paribas Targets Asian Super-Rich to Boost Wealth Business," Bloomberg, March 7, 2013.

5. "The Billionaires List," *Washington Post*, June 24, 2012.

billionaire's wealth. The 2001 list is used as the first period because data from 1997 to 2000 use a different methodology to assign wealth to family members, making it incomparable at the individual level to other years.[6]

Distinguishing Self-Made from Inherited Wealth

Each individual on the list was investigated to determine whether his or her wealth was self-made or inherited and to identify the industry and company primarily associated with the wealth and the gender of the individual. Wealth was considered self-made if the individual listed was the founder of the company or the source of wealth resulted from the person's position at a company. Billionaires who may have benefited from political connections or resource rents but did not inherit their wealth are also considered self-made.

Determining the extent to which wealth is inherited is more challenging than determining self-made wealth, because some billionaires inherited a fortune already in the billions when they entered the list while others built a smaller company into a billion-dollar one. In their analysis of the Forbes lists of the world's billionaires for 1987, 1992, 2001, and 2012, Kaplan and Rauh (2013) distinguish between billionaires whose wealth is self-made, inherited, and built from a "modest business." They find that inheritors of modest businesses make up less than 10 percent of total observations in both the United States and the world in 2012. They do not identify the cutoff for what constitutes a modest business.

In order to establish a clear cutoff, wealth is defined here as inherited if the 2014 billionaire is a relative of the founder of the company from which his or her primary source of wealth is derived. Using this definition provides a conservative estimate of self-made wealth and classifies billionaires who built smaller companies into billion-dollar ones in the inherited category. The most extreme example is Gina Rinehart, who built her $17.7 billion fortune from her father's $125 million mining business. In the methodology used, her wealth is considered inherited because she did not found the (still relatively large) company associated with her wealth.

The one exception is billionaires who inherited a single store or small factory from their family. These billionaires, who constitute about 2 percent of the sample, are considered self-made. They include GEMS Educa-

6. In 1996 and from 2001 to 2014, billionaires are reported as individuals. However, from 1997 to 2000, the list aggregates individual billionaires by family. As a result, the number of billionaires is systematically lower in these years and the average net worth of billionaires is systematically higher. These years can be used when considering aggregate net worth or examining wealth at the country or industry level; they cannot be used to analyze trends at the individual level, since this difference makes these years incomparable to later years.

tion chair Sunny Varkey, who took over a single school with fewer than 400 students from his parents and turned it into the largest operator of private K–12 schools in the world.[7]

The Forbes data report a billionaire's country by citizenship, as opposed to country of residence or birth. Using this citizenship variable, billionaires were divided into advanced countries and emerging markets. Countries in the first category include the high-income members of the Organization for Economic Cooperation and Development (OECD) at the beginning of the period (the United States and Canada, the countries of Western Europe, Australia, New Zealand, Japan, and Korea).[8] All other countries are grouped into the second category.

Figure 1.1 shows the share of billionaires by source of wealth in advanced countries and emerging markets in 2001 and 2014. Figure 1.2 shows the distribution of billionaire wealth. The number of billionaires and their wealth could be distributed differently if self-made billionaires are on average much wealthier than people who inherit their billions, who may split their fortunes with siblings.

Three facts emerge from these figures. First, even with this stringent view of inherited wealth, the majority of billionaires in both the advanced world and emerging markets are self-made. Second, the share of self-made billionaires remained broadly constant in the advanced world, at about 60 percent, but rose significantly in the developing world, reaching nearly 80 percent in 2014. Third, in each year and in each grouping, the percentage shares of the number of self-made billionaires and the aggregate value of their wealth are similar.

The share of billionaires that are self-made in 2014 is broadly consistent with research by Wealth-X, which estimates that 55 percent are self-made, 20 percent inherited their wealth, and 25 percent inherited some wealth and made the rest (Wealth-X and UBS 2014). The last category is defined as reaching "billionaire status through a combination of inheritance and hard work, either by starting their own business or taking an active role in their family businesses" (p. 25). The shares are roughly similar when the top of the distribution—where potential underreporting of inher-

---

7. For a detailed explanation of the methodology used to create these data, see Freund and Oliver (2016).

8. As a result of this decision, some high-income economies, including Taiwan and Singapore, are grouped in the South. Many of the billionaires and mega firms in these economies are from mainland China or produce in China or for the Chinese market. Wealthy Gulf nations are also classified as emerging markets. Although these countries are rich in oil, they have yet to experience the structural transformation that would qualify them as modern economies. Results remain qualitatively unchanged if these countries are not included in South.

**Figure 1.1   Share of self-made billionaires
in advanced economies and emerging
markets, 2001 and 2014** (percent)

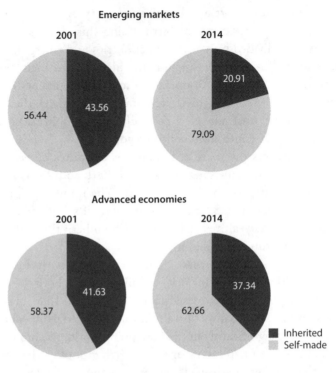

Emerging markets

| 2001 | 2014 |

2001: 56.44 / 43.56
2014: 20.91 / 79.09

Advanced economies

| 2001 | 2014 |

2001: 58.37 / 41.63
2014: 62.66 / 37.34

■ Inherited
■ Self-made

Source: Author's calculations using data from Forbes, The World's Billionaires, 2001, 2014.

ited wealth, which tends to be more diversified and hence harder to track, is likely to be less of an issue—is examined (Freund and Oliver 2016).

Classifying Billionaires Who Did Not Inherit Their Wealth

The superrich who did not inherit their wealth are classified into four broad categories: company founders, executives, government-connected or rent-related billionaires, and financial and real estate sector billionaires. This classification is likely to understate the size of the entrepreneurial class, because some of the winners of privatizations are highly skilled entrepreneurs who turned around weak state enterprises and many financial sector billionaires facilitated the development of new companies or helped create infrastructure for development. In addition, some billionaires who inherited wealth, such as Ratan Tata or Lee Kun-hee, presided over phenomenal company growth. Resource wealth may also benefit from leaders who

Figure 1.2   Share of self-made wealth among billionaires in advanced economies and emerging markets, 2001 and 2014
(percent)

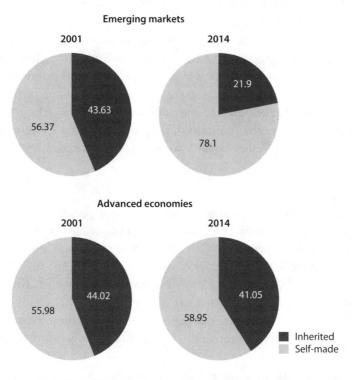

Source: Author's calculations using data from Forbes, The World's Billionaires, 2001, 2014.

make smart investment decisions, expanding scale, improving technology, and tightening the logistics of their companies.

Company Founders

Many billionaires become extraordinarily rich because of innovation, especially in fast-growing markets. Jan Koum and Brian Acton (combined net worth of $10 billion) of WhatsApp, a phone-based instant messaging service, first appeared on the list in 2014, after Facebook bought their app. Zhou Hongyi and Qi Xiangdong, of Qihoo 360, are together worth more than $3 billion. They captured the Chinese internet security market by offering their basic product free of charge and generating revenue through premium services. Both men appeared on the list for the first time in 2014.

Other billionaires got rich quickly with the help of political connections. Vagit Alekporov of Russia (worth $14 billion) was appointed deputy minister of oil and gas in 1990 and then catapulted into the lead position of Russia's largest private oil company, Lukoil, in 1991. Denis O'Brien of Ireland (worth $5.3 billion) won a valuable mobile phone license in 1995 with the aid of a politician.[9]

In order to conservatively estimate the number of company founders on the Forbes list who created innovative products, we exclude fortunes made in finance and real estate, natural resources, and political connections in the company founder category. Company founders thus most closely resemble the billionaires one thinks of as superstars: the people who invent new products that millions of people know and use or develop new production processes that expand varieties and reduce consumer prices.

Executives

A second category of self-made wealth includes people whose fortunes come from their position as an executive at a particular company (such as Facebook's Chief Operating Officer Sheryl Sandberg) that is not related to political connections, finance, or natural resources. Billionaires described as the chair, CEO, or other leader without also being listed as the founder are coded as executives in the dataset. This group also includes individuals who own a company but are not explicitly listed as a founder or given an executive title, such as billionaires who inherited a single store or factory.

Government-Connected or Rent-Related Billionaires

Fortunes stemming from political connections or natural resources are characterized as government connected or rent related.[10] A billionaire is identified as politically connected if there are news stories connecting his or her wealth to past positions in government, close relatives in government, or questionable licenses.

Also included in this category are self-made billionaires whose companies are privatized state-owned enterprises. By definition the acquisition of a state-owned company is connected to the government, as the trans-

---

9. Michael Moriarty, "Report of the Tribunal of Inquiry into Payments to Politicians and Related Matters, Part II," March 2011, www.moriarty-tribunal.ie/asp/detail.asp?objectid=3 10&Mode=0&RecordID=545.

10. Suthirtha Bagchi and Jan Svejnar (2013) also characterize the Forbes data according to political connections. If they find evidence, using Lexis Nexis searches, that the individual would not have become a billionaire in the absence of political connections, they deem the person to be politically connected.

Figure 1.3   Indices of real net worth of billionaires and energy price, 1996–2014

billionaire real net worth index, 1996=1   energy price index, 2010=100

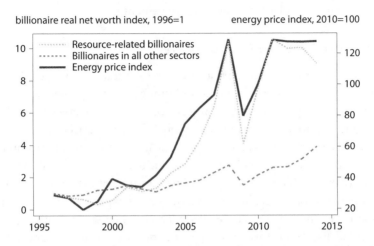

Sources: Data from World Bank, Global Economic Monitor (GEM) commodities database; and Forbes, The World's Billionaires.

action requires agreement from the government. Although privatization often results in better-managed firms, so some wealth accumulation is to be expected, this classification is made because the accumulation of $1 billion or more in wealth via privatization is suggestive of an underpriced deal. Rents accrued to the purchaser were likely more dependent on the company's business than the talent of the buyer.

Self-made billionaires whose wealth originates in resource-related in-dustries, including oil, natural gas, minerals, and coal, also fall into this category, because control over the area in which the resource is found is frequently determined through government contracts. Although some resource companies benefit from strong management, much of their re-turn is outside their control, a function of prices. The windfall of resource wealth is so well accepted that providence as opposed to skill was the ar-gument given in the recent divorce settlement of oil magnate Harold G. Hamm from Sue Ann Arnall. Hamm was not required to share half the wealth from his company, after more than 25 years of marriage, because his lawyers argued that the value of the company was a result of "passive" appreciation and not his ability as a CEO.[11]

The importance of external factors, as opposed to talent, in deter-mining resource wealth, is demonstrated in figure 1.3, which shows the

---

11. Robert Frank, "Are CEOs that Talented, or Just Lucky?" *New York Times*, February 8, 2015.

growth in total real net worth of resource-related billionaires compared with all other billionaires between 1996 and 2014.[12] The growth is nearly perfectly correlated with energy price movements.

Financial and Real Estate Sector Billionaires

Financial sector billionaires are also treated separately. Some of them, including investors who backed new and innovative companies early on, are superstars. Others benefited from political connections, weak regulatory oversight, and insider trading. The global financial crisis makes it especially hard to declare this group as genuine innovators, although some are. Many used brilliant strategies to channel much needed capital into high-growth firms, making big profits and promoting growth and jobs. Others found new ways of ensuring that markets are properly priced. The group of financial innovators includes Peter Thiel, a hedge fund manager who cofounded PayPal and was the first outside investor in Facebook; Bruce Kovner, the "inventor" of carry trade (the selling of currencies with low interest rates to buy currencies with high rates); and Petr Kellner of the Czech Republic, who developed Home Credit, a product that allows lower-middle-income individuals to access credit in 10 emerging markets, including Russia, India, Indonesia, China, Vietnam, and the Czech Republic.

Other financial-sector billionaires benefited from weak government oversight, sweetheart deals, and in some cases outright corruption. Michael Milken spent 22 months in prison for securities fraud but remains on the Forbes list, with assets of more than $2 billion.[13] Less well known but richer, with an estimated net wealth of nearly $10 billion, is Steven Cohen, the head of SAC Capital Advisors, a firm caught in a web of insider trading in 2013.[14] Indonesian investor Murdaya Poo managed to keep his fortune despite his wife's 2013 conviction of bribery to gain land concessions.[15]

---

12. Real net worth is the net worth of billionaires in 1996 US dollar terms. For an explanation of the methodology, see Freund and Oliver (2016).

13. Scott Cendrowski and James Bandler, "The SEC Is Investigating Michael Milken," *Fortune*, February 27, 2013, fortune.com/2013/02/27/the-sec-is-investigating-michael-milken.

14. Michael Rothfeld, "SAC Agrees to Plead Guilty in Insider-Trading Settlement," *Wall Street Journal*, November 4, 2013.

15. Ben Otto and Joko Hariyanto, "Indonesia Businesswoman Convicted of Graft," *Wall Street Journal*, February 4, 2013.

Wong Kwong Yu of China is serving 14 years in jail for insider trading and bribery.[16]

Also included in this category are real estate billionaires. Some benefited from government land concessions, others helped develop urban areas; many did both. China has the largest number of real estate tycoons in the South. They have promoted development by building the infrastructure that is supporting China's growth, but in a country where land is owned by the government and leased to the private sector, many are closely tied to politicians. The *New York Times* recently profiled the richest of the Chinese real estate moguls, Wang Jianlin, whose company, Wanda, is building skyscrapers, shopping malls, and theater complexes throughout China.[17] According to the *Times*, the elder sister of China's President Xi Jinping, the daughter of former prime minister Wen Jiabao, and relatives of former Politburo members all have large stakes in his multibillion-dollar company, though there is no evidence that they intervened on the company's behalf with the government.

Analysis

Table 1.1 shows the distribution of billionaires and their wealth across the five categories of billionaires in 2001 and 2014. The largest group within the self-made category in both years is company founders. The striking difference between 2001 and 2014 is the expansion in resource-related, privatization-related, and politically connected billionaires, whose share more than doubled in terms of both number and total wealth, at the expense of inherited wealth. There are notable differences between billionaires in the North and the South. Self-made billionaires in all categories except finance expanded their shares in emerging markets. In 2001, for example, just 12 percent of billionaires in emerging markets were company founders; by 2014 that figure had risen to 24 percent. The share of executives also jumped, from 5 to 11 percent. The shares of billionaires who owed their fortunes to government connections/rents or finance were flat. Shares changed less in advanced countries, where the greatest change was the small decline in inherited wealth and the concomitant increase in the shares of billionaires who got rich through finance or through government connections.

---

16. #149 Wong Kwong Yu and family, Forbes China Rich List, www.forbes.com/profile/wong-kwong-yu.

17. Michael Forsythe, "Billionaire at the Intersection of China's Business and Power," *New York Times*, April 29, 2015.

Table 1.1 Distribution of number and wealth of billionaires, by source of wealth, 2001 and 2014 (percent of total)

Source of wealth	Number of billionaires			Billionaire wealth		
	2001	2014	Contribution to growth, 2001–14	2001	2014	Contribution to growth, 2001–14
All regions						
Self-made	58.5	69.7	75.2	56.0	65.6	70.6
Company founder (nonfinance)	28.8	27.8	27.1	33.2	29.5	27.6
Owner or executive	8.2	9.2	10.2	5.5	6.0	6.3
Financial sector	16.9	21.5	23.6	13.5	18.1	20.5
Resource-related, privatization-related, or politically connected	4.6	11.2	14.3	3.8	12.0	16.2
Inherited	41.5	30.3	24.8	44.0	34.4	29.4
Emerging markets						
Self-made	56.3	79.1	82.9	56.4	78.1	81.8
Company founder (nonfinance)	11.6	23.8	25.9	7.4	21.9	24.3
Owner or executive	4.9	10.9	12.0	2.7	6.2	6.9
Financial sector	23.3	23.3	23.2	25.5	21.4	20.6
Resource-related, privatization-related, or politically connected	17.5	21.1	21.8	20.8	28.6	30.0
Inherited	42.7	20.9	17.1	43.6	21.9	18.2
Advanced economies						
Self-made	58.9	62.7	66.2	56.0	58.6	60.8
Company founder (nonfinance)	32.9	30.7	28.6	37.9	33.8	30.3
Owner or executive	9.0	8.0	8.1	6.0	6.0	5.9
Financial sector	15.4	20.1	23.7	11.4	16.2	20.3
Resource-related, privatization-related, or politically connected	1.6	3.9	5.8	0.7	2.6	4.3
Inherited	41.1	37.3	33.8	44.0	41.4	39.2

Source: Author's calculations using data from Forbes, The World's Billionaires.

Takeaways

Extreme wealth today is largely self-made, and the self-made share is growing, driven by emerging markets. Among self-made billionaires in emerging markets, the share of company founders and executives (excluding resource-based companies and privatized state enterprises) is growing exceptionally quickly, as the share of inherited money declines. The new emerging-market entrepreneur is one who builds a globally competitive mega firm, changing the economic landscape in his or her home country.

The picture is less dynamic in the North, although the share of inherited wealth is declining there, too. A worrisome trend is that it is being replaced by politically connected wealth and wealth from finance rather than wealth created by founders of firms.

2

Billionaires, by Region and Sector

Billionaire wealth in emerging markets has been growing much faster than wealth in the advanced countries in recent years. A great deal of this wealth has accrued to founders of big global companies—people like Cyrus Poonawalla of India, whose Serum Institute makes more polio vaccine than any other company in the world, and Miguel Krigsner, who owns Grupo Boticario, Brazil's second-largest cosmetics company. Most emerging markets have produced this new breed of highly productive businessmen, but some regions and countries have outperformed others.

East Asia is especially dynamic, with 115 company founders (excluding finance and real estate) in 2014. Many are well-known individuals, like Terry Gou, the founder of Foxconn, which makes iPads, and Jack Ma, the founder of Alibaba, the online marketplace. Many of the new companies are competing in the tradable sector and in new sectors (relatively contestable industries), not in resources and telecoms, as in the past. Political connections and resources are still mainstays of extraordinary wealth in Latin America and emerging Europe, but even there the number of company founders has grown. Even Africa, where a decade ago all wealth was inherited, has a growing share of company founders. Many, like Christoffel Wiese, the founder of Pepkor, a clothing retailer in Africa, are from South Africa.

Such self-made founders account for an increasing share of wealth in emerging-market regions, with the important exceptions of the Middle East and North Africa (MENA) and South Asia. In South Asia great fortunes associated with political connections and finance have been on the rise, and MENA is increasingly dominated by inheritance. These trends in regions known for their failure to integrate into the global economy are disturbing.

This chapter examines how billionaire wealth varies across sectors and regions. It also identifies the industries in which billionaires are concentrated.

Billionaire Data around the Globe

The real net worth of the world's billionaires increased rapidly between 1996 and 2014 (figure 2.1). The rapid growth in real net worth in emerging markets began in the mid-2000s; earlier growth centered in the advanced countries. Both advanced countries and emerging markets experienced a sharp drop in total net worth in 2009, but by 2014 the total real net worth of billionaires exceeded 2008 levels for both groups.

Figure 2.1 Total real net worth of billionaires in advanced economies and emerging markets, 1996–2014

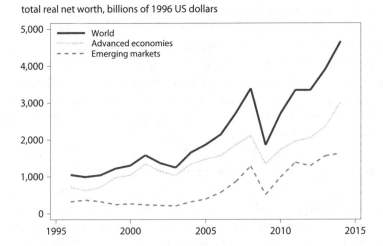

total real net worth, billions of 1996 US dollars

Sources: Data from Forbes, The World's Billionaires; and World Bank, *World Development Indicators.*

Which Sectors Account for This Growth?

Wealth comes from five broad sectors: resource related, new, traded, nontraded, and financial. Table 2.1 identifies the major industry categories in each sector.

The resource-related sector includes all natural resources as well as steel. Steel is included in this category because the key inputs needed for its production (coal and iron ore) are major components of the resource sec-

Table 2.1 Sector classification

Sector	Industries
Resource-related	Energy (excluding wind and solar), mining, and steel
New	Computer technology, software, medical technology, solar and wind energy, and pharmaceuticals
Nontraded	Retail, entertainment, media, construction, telecom, restaurants, and other service industries
Traded	Agriculture, consumer goods, shipping, and manufacturing
Financial	Banking, insurance, hedge funds, private equity, venture capital, investments, diversified wealth, and real estate
Other[a]	Education, engineering, infrastructure, and sports team ownership

a. Accounts for less than 5 percent of observations.

Table 2.2 Distribution of number and wealth of billionaires, by sector, 1996 and 2014 (percent of total)

	Number of billionaires			Billionaire wealth		
Sector	1996	2014	Contribution to increase, 1996–2014	1996	2014	Contribution to increase, 1996–2014
Emerging economies						
Resource-related	8.3	16.2	18.0	7.1	21.9	25.5
New	0	10.9	13.4	0	9.1	11.3
Nontraded	18.2	16.2	15.8	13.4	17.0	17.9
Traded	22.7	19.3	18.5	19.4	17.1	16.5
Financial	48.5	35.5	32.5	59.0	34.0	27.9
Other	2.3	1.9	1.8	1.1	0.9	0.9
Advanced countries						
Resource-related	5.2	6.7	7.4	4.1	4.8	5.0
New	12.4	13.9	14.6	17.0	16.6	16.5
Nontraded	29.2	23.4	20.8	29.0	26.5	25.7
Traded	25.1	23.6	22.9	25.4	24.0	23.6
Financial	24.7	28.2	29.7	22.3	25.2	26.1
Other	3.4	4.2	4.6	2.2	2.9	3.1

Source: Data from Forbes, The World's Billionaires.

tor. The "new" sector captures the effect of changing computer and medical technology on billionaire wealth. Traded sectors are separated from nontraded sectors in order to assess the impact of trade openness and globalization. Construction is considered a nontraded sector. Real estate is grouped in the financial sector, because real estate investment more closely resembles an asset than a good or service for consumption.

Table 2.3   Countries in each regional group, 1996–2014

Group	Countries/economies
Anglo countries	Australia, Canada, New Zealand, United States
Latin America	Argentina, Belize, Brazil, Chile, Colombia, Ecuador, Mexico, Peru, St. Kitts and Nevis, Venezuela
Europe	
High-income	Austria, Belgium, Denmark, Finland, France, Germany, Greece, Iceland, Ireland, Italy, Liechtenstein, Monaco, Netherlands, Norway, Portugal, Spain, Sweden, Switzerland, United Kingdom
Emerging-market	Cyprus, Czech Republic, Georgia, Lithuania, Poland, Romania, Russia, Serbia, Ukraine
Sub-Saharan Africa	Angola, Nigeria, South Africa, Swaziland, Tanzania, Uganda
Middle East and North Africa	Algeria, Bahrain, Egypt, Israel, Kuwait, Lebanon, Morocco, Oman, Qatar, Saudi Arabia, Turkey, United Arab Emirates
South Asia	India, Kazakhstan, Nepal, Pakistan
East Asia	
High-income	Japan, South Korea
Emerging-market	China, Hong Kong, Indonesia, Macau, Malaysia, Philippines, Singapore, Thailand, Taiwan, Vietnam

Table 2.2 (located on page 33) shows how billionaires and their wealth are distributed across sectors. In emerging markets, finance was responsible for 60 percent of billionaire wealth in 1996; by 2014 its share had fallen to 34 percent. In contrast, in the advanced countries, sectoral shares were relatively stable.

Regional Trends: From East Asia to Africa

In 1996, 40 countries were represented on the billionaires list; by 2014 the figure had grown to 69. These billionaires come from one of seven regions: Europe (separated into high-income and emerging-market countries), Latin America, sub-Saharan Africa, MENA, South and Central Asia, East Asia (separated into high-income and emerging-market countries), and Anglo countries (the United States, Canada, Australia, and New Zealand). See table 2.3 for countries/economies included in each category. Billionaire wealth is concentrated in Europe, East Asia, and the Anglo countries (figure 2.2). Sub-Saharan Africa has the smallest share of total real billionaire net worth.

Within emerging markets, East Asian billionaires represent the largest group in terms of total real net worth, except between 2006 and 2008, when emerging Europe dominated. Following the global financial crisis, East Asian, Latin American, and European billionaire wealth rebounded quickly. In contrast, wealth in South and Central Asia and MENA stagnated or declined. Billionaire wealth in sub-Saharan Africa increased slightly after 2010.

Figure 2.2 Total real net worth of billionaires, by region, 1996–2014

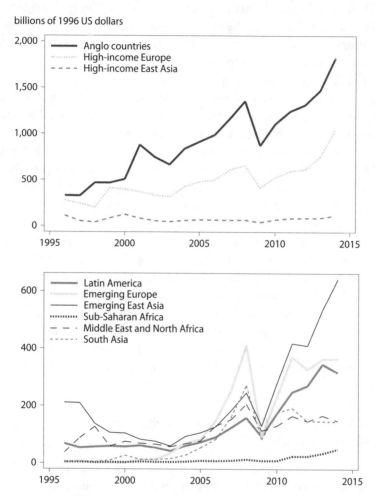

billions of 1996 US dollars

Sources: Data from Forbes, The World's Billionaires; and World Bank, *World Development Indicators*.

East Asia: Land of Big Business

East Asian billionaires are by far the most dynamic group. Many Chinese billionaires have been able to take advantage of the large Chinese market for specific goods. Robin Li's search engine, Baidu, for example, reaped more than 99 percent of its revenue within China in 2013. Some billionaires built their fortunes through trade, such as waste paper queen Cheung Yan, who imports recycled paper from the United States and turns it into packaging for Chinese exports. Others built their fortunes by bringing existing products to the region. The company owned by Indonesia's Achmad Hamami, for example, controls the manufacturing and sale of Caterpillar equipment in Indonesia. Other entrepreneurs—such as Tony Tan, the founder of the Philippine fast-food restaurant Jollibee—created companies that serve local markets before expanding regionally.

Thanks to this new group of company founders, there has been an enormous shift in the countries and industries represented in the billionaire group. In terms of countries, billionaires from mainland Chinese are the big story. The Chinese moved from being unrepresented on the Forbes list in 1996 to making up more than 40 percent of East Asian billionaires in 2014. The rise of China is reflected in the change in the shares of inherited and self-made wealth. In 2001 more than 40 percent of East Asian billionaires inherited their fortunes; by 2014 the share of inheritors in emerging Asia had fallen to 12 percent (table 2.4).[1]

The other major change was in the financial sector. The Asian financial crisis of 1997 decimated many financial sector fortunes, replacing them with more diverse sources of wealth. In 1996 there were 69 emerging-market East Asian billionaires, 64 percent of them from countries in the Association of Southeast Asian Nations (ASEAN) (Indonesia, Malaysia, the Philippines, Singapore, and Thailand).[2] By 2014 the share of ASEAN billionaires had dropped to less than half of the total in East Asia. New industries and tradables had replaced finance in emerging East Asia (table 2.5).

Latin America: Still High Levels of Inherited Wealth but Growing Shares of Innovators

Latin America is unique among emerging-market regions in beginning the period with over 60 percent of the billionaire population as inherited wealth. With a combined net worth of $12.5 billion, the six billionaire heirs to the Votorantim Group, which was founded as a textile factory in 1919 and later became the first Brazilian chemical company, reflect the importance of inherited wealth in Latin America.

But things are changing. By 2014 the inherited share had fallen to 49 percent (table 2.4). Inheritors are being replaced by Latin American innovators who have taken advantage of global markets to grow their companies.

---

1. China had a single billionaire in 2001, Rong Yiren, former vice president and founder of state-owned investment corporation CITIC Group.

2. The remaining third were from Taiwan and Hong Kong.

Table 2.4   Distribution of billionaires, by source of wealth and region, 2001 and 2014 (percent of total)

Region	2001	2014		2001	2014
			Emerging markets		
East Asia			**Middle East and North Africa**		
Self-made wealth	59.4	88.2	Self-made wealth	63.6	56.4
Company founder (nonfinance)	10.8	31.0	Company founder (nonfinance)	22.7	17.9
Owner or executive	5.4	16.8	Owner or executive	4.6	9.0
Financial sector	32.4	29.6	Financial sector	22.7	15.4
Resource-related, privatization-related, or politically connected	10.8	10.8	Resource-related, privatization-related, or politically connected	13.6	14.1
Inherited wealth	40.6	11.8	Inherited wealth	36.4	43.6
Number of billionaires	37	297	Number of billionaires	22	78
Latin America			**South Asia**		
Self-made wealth	39.3	50.9	Self-made wealth	50.0	69.4
Company founder (nonfinance)	3.6	19.3	Company founder (nonfinance)	50.0	30.7
Owner or executive	0	6.1	Owner or executive	0	6.5
Financial sector	25.0	16.7	Financial sector	0	14.5
Resource-related, privatization-related, or politically connected	10.7	8.8	Resource-related, privatization-related, or politically connected	0	17.7
Inherited wealth	60.7	49.1	Inherited wealth	50.0	30.6
Number of billionaires	28	114	Number of billionaires	4	62
Europe			**Sub-Saharan Africa**		
Self-made wealth	100	100	Self-made wealth	0	81.3
Company founder (nonfinance)	0	12.3	Company founder (nonfinance)	0	25.0
Owner or executive	11.1	4.4	Owner or executive	0	18.8
Financial sector	0	24.6	Financial sector	0	12.5
Resource-related, privatization-related, or politically connected	88.9	58.7	Resource-related, privatization-related, or politically connected	0	25.0
Inherited wealth	0	0	Inherited wealth	100	18.7
Number of billionaires	9	138	Number of billionaires	2	16

(table continues)

Table 2.4   Distribution of billionaires, by source of wealth and region, 2001 and 2014 (percent of total) *(continued)*

	2001	2014
Advanced economies		
Anglo countries		
Self-made wealth	64.0	71.3
Company founder (nonfinance)	34.3	31.3
Owner or executive	9.3	8.7
Financial sector	19.0	27.2
Resource-related, privatization-related, or politically connected	1.4	4.1
Inherited wealth	36.0	28.7
Number of billionaires	289	562
Europe		
Self-made wealth	48.3	49.4
Company founder (nonfinance)	28.7	28.0
Owner or executive	9.6	7.2
Financial sector	6.1	10.0
Resource-related, privatization-related, or politically connected	2.6	4.2
Inherited wealth	53.0	50.6
Number of billionaires	115	332
East Asia		
Self-made wealth	54.8	53.7
Company founder (nonfinance)	35.5	40.7
Owner or executive	3.2	5.6
Financial sector	16.1	7.4
Resource-related, privatization-related, or politically connected	0	0
Inherited wealth	45.2	46.3
Number of billionaires	31	54

Source: Data from Forbes, The World's Billionaires.

Table 2.5 Distribution of number and wealth of billionaires, by sector and region, 1996 and 2014 (percent of total)

Region/sector	Number of billionaires			Billionaire wealth		
	1996	2014	Contribution to growth, 1996–2014	1996	2014	Contribution to growth, 1996–2014
Emerging markets						
Latin America						
Resource-related	12.5	13.2	13.5	12.7	14.4	14.9
New	0	1.8	2.7	0	1.2	1.5
Nontraded	32.5	22.8	17.6	34.6	34.6	34.7
Traded	32.5	27.2	24.3	33.2	26.0	24.0
Financial	20.0	33.3	40.5	17.9	23.2	24.6
Other	2.5	1.7	1.4	1.6	0.6	0.3
Europe						
Resource-related	0	38.0	38.2	0	55.8	56.1
New	0	1.5	1.5	0	0.7	0.7
Nontraded	100	17.5	16.9	100	13.1	12.7
Traded	0	10.9	11.0	0	8.7	8.7
Financial	0	31.4	31.6	0	20.9	20.9
Other	0	0.7	0.8	0	0.8	0.9
Sub-Saharan Africa						
Resource-related	50	25.0	21.4	60.9	19.3	15.5
New	0	6.2	7.2	0	1.9	2.1
Nontraded	0	37.5	42.9	0	56.9	62.1
Traded	50	12.5	7.1	39.0	12.9	10.5
Financial	0	18.8	21.4	0	8.9	9.8
Other	0	0	0	0	0	0
Middle East and North Africa						
Resource-related	0	11.5	14.8	0	16.7	21.9
New	0	9.0	11.5	0	4.7	6.2
Nontraded	17.6	24.4	26.2	19.9	21.4	21.9
Traded	17.7	10.2	8.2	15.6	10.4	8.7
Financial	64.7	43.6	37.7	64.5	45.9	40.1
Other	0	1.3	1.6	0	0.9	1.2

(table continues)

Table 2.5 Distribution of number and wealth of billionaires, by sector and region, 1996 and 2014 (percent of total) *(continued)*

Region/sector	Number of billionaires			Billionaire wealth		
	1996	2014	Contribution to growth, 1996–2014	1996	2014	Contribution to growth, 1996–2014
South Asia						
Resource-related	66.6	19.4	17.0	76.6	31.0	29.4
New	0	25.8	27.1	0	31.8	32.9
Nontraded	0	12.9	13.6	0	11.0	11.4
Traded	33.3	17.7	16.9	23.4	10.0	9.5
Financial	0	19.4	20.3	0	14.0	14.5
Other	0	4.8	5.1	0	2.2	2.3
East Asia						
Resource-related	4.4	7.4	8.3	3.9	5.6	6.5
New		16.5	21.5	0	14.1	21.0
Nontraded	10.1	10.5	10.5	5.4	7.8	9.0
Traded	17.4	23.2	25.0	15.3	21.0	23.8
Financial	65.2	40.4	32.9	74.2	50.5	38.8
Other	2.9	2.0	1.8	1.2	1.0	0.9
Advanced economies						
Anglo countries						
Resource-related	9.2	7.2	6.5	7.4	5.7	5.3
New	11.4	14.9	16.2	17.6	19.8	20.3
Nontraded	31.9	20.7	16.9	31.1	24.1	22.6
Traded	24.1	16.6	14.0	27.0	15.1	12.4
Financial	21.3	36.8	42.3	15.4	33.6	37.6
Other	2.1	3.8	4.1	1.5	1.7	1.8
Europe						
Resource-related	1.0	6.9	9.6	0.9	3.8	4.9
New	12.6	9.0	7.4	18.2	8.7	5.3
Nontraded	31.1	25.9	23.6	31.2	29.4	28.7
Traded	29.1	36.5	39.7	28.0	40.5	48.8
Financial	21.4	16.6	14.4	18.1	12.4	10.3
Other	4.8	5.1	5.3	3.6	5.2	5.8

(table continues)

Table 2.5 Distribution of number and wealth of billionaires, by sector and region, 1996 and 2014 (percent of total) *(continued)*

	Number of billionaires			Billionaire wealth		
Region/sector	1996	2014	Contribution to growth, 1996–2014	1996	2014	Contribution to growth, 1996–2014
East Asia						
Resource-related	2.1	0	−14.3	2.1	0	−24.4
New	14.9	33.3	171.4	12.5	36.8	1,085.60
Nontraded	17.0	35.2	157.2	17.3	38.9	972.6
Traded	19.1	16.7	0	14.3	15.8	82.6
Financial	42.6	11.1	−200.0	51.7	7.1	−1,920.1
Other	4.3	3.7	−14.3	2.1	1.4	−296.3

Source: Data from Forbes, The World's Billionaires.

Brazilian Alexandre Grendene Bartelle is an example. His shoe company, Grendene, which produces low-cost footwear for both the domestic and international markets, is the world's largest sandal maker. In Peru four of the five self-made billionaires on the 2014 list are company founders.

For Latin American billionaires, the nontraded sectors, particularly retail, media and telecommunications, and construction, initially captured the largest share of billionaire wealth, together accounting for about one-third of such wealth (table 2.5). Finance has taken over the lead over the last decade, while most other sectors have contributed to growth with roughly stable shares. One exception is the new sectors, which grew somewhat but still generated less than 2 percent of extreme wealth in 2014.

Brazil looks like the rest of Latin America, with high levels of inheritance, especially compared with the other BRICs (table 2.6). Founders and executives make up about one-third of all billionaires in Brazil, and their numbers are growing.

Emerging Europe: Home of the Self-Made Billionaire

High-income and emerging Europe diverge. Wealth in emerging Europe is steadily moving away from nontradables into other sectors. In contrast, high-income Europe has seen little change in the share of wealth in each sector over time (table 2.5).

The big difference is in inherited wealth (table 2.4). There are no family dynasties in emerging Europe. In contrast, wealth in old Europe is largely old money. Europe as a whole is divided about evenly between self-made

Table 2.6 Sources of wealth of billionaires in BRIC countries, 2001 and 2014 (percent of total)

Country	2001	2014	Country	2001	2014
Brazil			**India**		
Self-made wealth	33.3	52.3	Self-made wealth	100	66.1
Company founder (nonfinance)	0	21.5	Company founder (nonfinance)	50	33.9
Owner or executive	0	7.7	Owner or executive	0	7.2
Financial sector	33.3	18.5	Financial sector	0	14.3
Resource-related, privatization-related, or politically connected	0	4.6	Resource-related, privatization-related, or politically connected	50	10.7
Inherited wealth	66.7	47.7	Inherited wealth	0	33.9
Number of billionaires	6	65	Number of billionaires	4	56
Russia			**China**		
Self-made wealth	100	100	Self-made wealth	100	98
Company founder (nonfinance)	0	10.8	Company founder (nonfinance)	0	40.1
Owner or executive	0	3.6	Owner or executive	0	25.0
Financial sector		22.5	Financial sector	0	23.7
Resource-related, privatization-related, or politically connected	100	63.1	Resource-related, privatization-related, or politically connected	100	9.2
Inherited wealth	0	0	Inherited wealth	0	2.0
Number of billionaires	8	111	Number of billionaires	1	152

Source: Data from Forbes, The World's Billionaires.

and inherited wealth. Emerging Europe is dominated by resource rents, but like other emerging markets there is rapid growth in the number of company founders.

Many billionaires in emerging Europe were able to take advantage of the wave of privatization following the fall of the Soviet Union. Ukraine's president, Petro Poroshenko, built his confectionery empire by first creating a small private company and then acquiring cheap Soviet candy factories. Others took advantage of the transition as first movers in new sectors. Entrepreneur Zygmunt Solorz-Zak benefited from the transformation of the media sector, establishing one of the first private television companies in Poland.

Russia has more resource-related/politically connected wealth than any of the other BRICs (table 2.6). As the oil magnate Vladimir Yevtushenkov commented, "The size of your business should be matched by the size of your political influence. If your political influence is smaller than

Figure 2.3   Sources of wealth of Arab billionaires, 2001 and 2014 (percent)

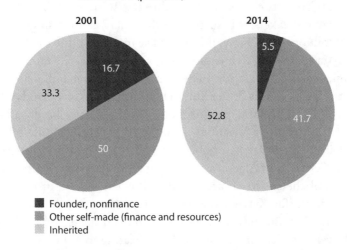

2001

2014

16.7

33.3

50

5.5

52.8

41.7

■ Founder, nonfinance
▨ Other self-made (finance and resources)
▨ Inherited

Note: All Forbes data exclude royals.
Source: Data from Forbes, The World's Billionaires.

your business, it will be taken away from you. If your political influence is bigger than your business, then you are a politician."[3] Founders still represent a small share of Russian billionaires, but their numbers grew markedly in the 2000s. Outside Russia the number of billionaires in emerging Europe is now roughly evenly split among resource- and privatization-related billionaires, financial-sector billionaires, and founders.

Middle East and North Africa: Growing Shares of Inherited Wealth, Declining Entrepreneurship

MENA is the only emerging-market region in which the share of inherited wealth has increased over time and the share of founders decreased. Self-made MENA billionaires are highly dependent on resource-related and politically connected wealth. Table 2.4 overstates company founders, because Turkey and Israel, two outliers, are included in MENA.[4] Excluding them, the share of founders falls to less than 6 percent in 2014, one-third of the share in 2001 (figure 2.3).

---

3. "Billionaire Placed under House Arrest in Russia," *New York Times*, September 18, 2014.

4. Israel is included in emerging markets because it was not a member of the Organization for Economic Cooperation and Development (OECD) until 2010. Including it in the advanced-country group does not significantly affect any of the results, with the exception of MENA region aggregates, as discussed in this section.

Something in the region, especially the Arabic-speaking part, is preventing large private companies from thriving. With more than 300 million native Arabic speakers, it is surprising that there is not a single computer industry billionaire. (China and India have many, and the founder of Yandex, Russia's largest search engine, is a billionaire despite a much smaller Russian-speaking population.) There are only two Arab billionaires in consumer tradables. One is Prince Sultan bin Mohammed bin Saud Al Kabeer, whose company, Almarai, produces dairy in the desert—hardly a business based on comparative advantage. The other is Algeria's only billionaire, Issad Rebrab, a teacher before he switched to business in the 1970s and founded Cevital, now Algeria's largest sugar exporter. In the rest of MENA, the ranks of the superrich are populated by the second or third generations of wealthy families like the Hariris of Lebanon and the Mansours and Sawiris of Egypt. Businessmen and -women from the region have done extremely well in other parts of the world, indicating that the issue is not people but the climate for investment and commerce in the region. The most well-known is Mo Ibrahim, born in Sudan and now a British citizen, who started the African mobile phone company Celtel, which had tens of millions of subscribers when he sold for $3.5 billion. Nicolas Hayek, of Lebanon, was a cofounder of the phenomenally successful company Swatch. This was Hayek's second highly productive venture in Switzerland, the first was Hayek Engineering, a prosperous management consulting firm. The Syrian-born French entrepreneur Mohed Altrad turned a bankrupt scaffolding company into a billion-dollar one. Having grown up Bedouin in the desert of Syria, his story is one of rags to riches, after receiving a scholarship to study abroad.

The sectors responsible for wealth in MENA have also changed little over time: Finance and nontradables continue to drive wealth, very little of which is generated by new sectors or tradables. These sectors are concentrated in Israel and Turkey. Resources show up only in the later years, not because they were not important in prior years but because resource wealth has traditionally been confined to the ruling class, who by construction are not included in the Forbes data.

Sub-Saharan Africa: Showing Signs of Change

Resource-related wealth dominated the period 1996–2011 in sub-Saharan Africa. But in recent years traded sector wealth, spurred in large part by the fortune of Nigerian tycoon Aliko Dangote, surpassed resource-related wealth, as Dangote transformed his trading company into a producer of flour, sugar, and cement that operates throughout West Africa.

South Africa is home to half of the billionaires of the region, with all of the region's inherited wealth and nearly 40 percent of self-made wealth. Billionaires from other countries (including Angola, Nigeria, Swaziland, Tanzania, and Uganda) tend to be founders and company executives.

South Asia: Innovation in India, Resource- and Government-Related Wealth Elsewhere in the Region

Resources remain an important source of wealth in South Asia. By 2014, however, new industries made up a larger share of wealth than resource-related industries, driven by falling commodity prices and the rise of Indian computer and pharmaceutical billionaires.[5] The two sectors each account for about 40 percent of billionaire wealth. Four of the six founders of Infosys, an Indian company that creates software and provides information technology services primarily for the banking sector, were on the billionaires list in 2014. A complex program of allocating resource permits in India has also allowed the rise of rent-related resource billionaires.

Outside India, Nepal's Binod Chaudhary is the only billionaire in the region not connected to resources or the government. Chaudhary turned his father's department store, the first in Nepal, into an international conglomerate by marketing products, such as its popular instant noodles, regionally rather than exclusively for his small home market.

Takeaways

Sources of wealth differ across the emerging-market world. East Asia is the most dynamic emerging region, with an enormous amount of self-made wealth, most of which is accruing to company founders. Latin America has large shares of inherited wealth relative to the rest of the world. Emerging European countries (particularly Russia) have high levels of politically connected wealth. In Latin America, MENA, emerging Europe, and South Asia, resource-related sectors and political connections remain important, although except in MENA and South Asia, the share of rentiers is on the decline and the share of company founders growing.

---

5. Aditi Gandhi and Michael Walton (2012) note this trend in Indian billionaire wealth using Forbes data through 2012. The analysis in this book is consistent with their findings, revealing the continued decrease in the influence of rent seekers among Indian billionaires.

II

THEIR BUSINESSES

3

Why Are Large Firms
Good for Growth?

In the ideal world of many philosophers since ancient times, individuals and groups should be rewarded economically for their enterprise—but not excessively so. But modernization in what is today the developed world enriched a new class of superwealthy in a pattern that is now being repeated in less developed countries. The rise of a class of extremely wealthy individuals in less affluent countries can be offensive in the sight of those who work hard with less reward. But this chapter mobilizes research to show that the rise of a superrich category of people in emerging markets is a natural and inevitable part of development and modernization because they are also the people who create the mega firms that transform an economy. This chapter argues that large private firms and the entrepreneurs that lead them increase the efficiency of resource allocation in a country. In terms of production, value added, and wages, one highly productive firm with 10,000 employees making apparel is more beneficial than 1,000 firms with 10 employees. Development is spurred the most when resources are drawn to the best firms. Like it or not, that leads to the dominance of a few highly successful companies and individuals. Thus the emergence of rich people and rich companies in poor countries is a reflection of a healthy economy.

The growing number of emerging-market company founders is driven by the growing number of emerging-market mega firms. In 1996 less than 3 percent of global Fortune 500 companies were from emerging markets. In 2014 nearly 30 percent were. Emerging-market firms also made up 30 percent of the 2014 Forbes Global 2000 list of largest companies, twice their share in 2007.[1] Twenty percent of emerging-market billionaires are directly connected to firms on the Forbes Global 2000 list.

The takeoff of large companies from emerging markets led the *Financial Times* to launch an Emerging Market 500 list in 2011. The firms on the 2014 list had a combined market value of $7.5 trillion, net income of $706 billion, and more than 19 million employees. Their net income was equivalent to that of more than 30 Microsofts.

Many of the top companies in emerging markets have historically been in resources and finance and benefited from political connections. A traditional example of a company-billionaire connection is Reliance Industries the most profitable company in India, which is connected to Mukesh Ambani, India's richest man. Reliance is in the business of resources and telecommunications. Another classic example is Halyk Bank of Kazakhstan, working in investments and retail banking, connected to Timur Kulibaev, the son-in-law of Kazakh president Nursultan Nazarbayev.

But the rise of relatively young manufacturers and tech firms without such helpful political and family connections is notable. One-third of the emerging-market billionaires who made their fortunes in a firm now in the top 2000 are company founders. This figure is higher than the share of company founders in the overall list.

Near the top of the list is Foxconn, China's largest exporter, which employs nearly 1 million people. Like Steve Jobs, Foxconn's founder, Terry Gou, got his start working for Atari. After starting a company with $7,500 and a few friends in 1974, he won his first big contract in 1980, making parts for Atari. From there Gou quickly pivoted from plastic parts to patents and technology. After the Atari deal, he knocked on the doors of all the top US companies, hanging around until he got a big order. Some business journalists have compared the revolution in supply chains for electronics that he initiated to the revolution Ford achieved with the assembly line.[2]

The Brazilian company WEG—founded by an electrician, a manager, and a mechanic, whose first initials form the company name—started by producing electric motors. It has since moved into other areas, including industrial automation. It has manufacturing plants in Brazil as well as other parts of Latin America, China, and India.

Bharat Forge, of India, a manufacturer of auto parts and metal forgings for machines, earns most of its revenues from overseas sales. Baba

---

1. Forbes measures size, weighting revenues, assets, profits, and market valuation equally.

2. Frederik Balfour and Tim Culpan, "The Man Who Makes Your iPhone," *Bloomberg Business*, September 9, 2010.

Kalyani, its chair, transformed the small firm his father started, which had annual turnover of less than $2 million, into a company valued at more than $2 billion. Before the 1990s the firm's business was mainly with Russia. Economic reform allowed the firm to compete more broadly. It now supplies auto industry leaders like Audi, Mercedes, and Ford.

This breed of large and fast-growing companies is exactly what economic researchers would expect to see in a successful economy. Productivity gains are the main source of improvements in living standards. The availability of firm-level data has made it possible to disaggregate productivity growth into its various components. Research shows that the allocation of resources between firms in narrowly defined industries is a major factor in productivity growth (Bartelsman and Doms 2000; Foster, Haltiwanger, and Krizan 2001). When the business climate allows the most productive firms to grow rapidly, they attract resources away from less productive firms. As a result, output expands. As economies develop, large highly productive firms tend to employ a greater share of the labor force and account for a growing share of value added in an economy.

The empirical literature reveals three pertinent findings. First, there are numerous small firms for every large firm, but large firms account for a huge share of production, jobs, and trade. Second, the ability of high-productivity firms to grow explains a great deal of country productivity. Third, large firms and startups are generally responsible for net job creation. When resources move to the most competitive firms in the industry, countries grow faster. In some industries larger firms are a necessity in order to take advantage of returns to scale. (Car producers, for example, are typically inefficient at less than 200,000 units per plant a year.)

The ability of firms to grow large also helps individuals amass huge fortunes. Growth and development, whether at the country or the industry level, are thus likely to favor large highly productive firms and lead to extreme wealth. In a political context, the dominance of such firms and the influence of wealthy individuals might be controversial, but such a development can be beneficial for a nation's economic efficiency and growth. To the extent that large-scale entrepreneurs face competition, they drive resources to their most productive uses and expand profits. In advanced and flexible economies like the United States and the United Kingdom, for example, the largest or fastest-growing firms tend to be the most productive in the industry. The emergence of fast-growing productive firms that generate large profits can benefit emerging markets in particular, because entrepreneurs are likely to be much better intermediaries of capital than governments. In addition, wealth concentration in regions that lack deep financial markets may make the big investments needed for industrialization more feasible.

That said, the presence of a few large firms is not always an indicator of efficient resource allocation. Especially where business regulations are cumbersome and firms are shielded from international competition, unproductive large firms can dominate a market, depressing growth. These large firms will look different from the dynamic ones because they will not be especially productive nor will they tend to compete in contested markets. Such anticompetitive big business stymies growth. Only when size and productivity move together is size an indicator of allocative efficiency.

Overall, the gains by emerging-market firms in global markets are consistent with improved allocative efficiency, as many of the new large firms are competing in global markets, and exporting firms are very likely to be among the most competitive in a country.

Firm Size and Allocation of Resources among Firms

Richer countries are richer because they produce more goods and services for each employed worker. Traditional thinking among many economists has been that workers produce more output in developed countries because they have more capital, better technology, and better skills. But it turns out that access to capital, technology, and skills only partly explains the success stories of developed countries. Economists then turned to resource allocation between industries. Putting capital and labor in the sectors where they are most productive contributes significantly to growth. But that was not the end of the story. Resource allocation among firms within industries is even more important for growth and development. Firms are very different, even in the same country within narrowly defined industries. Studies typically find that a firm in the 90th percentile of productivity is many times more productive than a firm in the 10th percentile: Using the same inputs, a firm at the top of the distribution produces about four to five times as much as a firm at the bottom.[3]

Despite these vast differences between firms, the earlier growth literature assumed a representative firm, whose resource use and productivity were replicated many times. This eliminated resource allocation between

---

3. Using data from the 1977 US manufacturing census, Chad Syverson (2004) finds that a firm in the 90th percentile in a four-digit Standard Industrial Classification industry (443 industries) is on average four times as productive as a firm in the 10th percentile, with several US industries seeing much wider differences. This gap widens as one moves out in the distribution: A firm in the 95th percentile is seven times as productive as a firm in the 5th percentile. Productivity differences tend to be even larger in developing countries (Hsieh and Klenow 2009).

firms as a source of growth. But in all countries, there are many small firms and a few large firms, with large firms dominating markets for many goods and services. In Mexico, for example, Walmex controls by far the largest share of Mexico's supermarket business, but numerous smaller chains and individually owned stores compete as well. In China, Alibaba dominates ecommerce, just as Amazon dominates it in the United States though many specialty sites exist. And country superstars are often global superstars. Anheuser-Busch and Samsung each have over 20 percent of the world markets for beer and smart phones, respectively. Toyota, GM, and VW together share one third of the global market for cars.

One reason why richer countries are able to produce more goods and services is that they use their resources more efficiently. Highly productive firms in particular absorb a disproportionate share of resources, raising output levels. In contrast, in developing countries the largest firms are not always the most productive. This misallocation of resources among firms is a critical element explaining why poor countries are poor and why growth stalls in many middle-income countries. Wide heterogeneity in firm performance, which is common in most developing markets, is taken as an indicator of resource misallocation. The intuition is that the most productive firms should absorb most resources, grow large, and hence be relatively similar in performance.

An even more precise indicator of allocative efficiency is the covariance between firm size and productivity. An economy is more productive when more efficient firms have a larger and increasing share of activity. If firm performance and size are uncorrelated, resources are not being pulled into their most productive uses.

Consider the following example. Imagine the Chinese steel industry has two firms, each with 100 workers. The first firm produces three units of steel per worker, and the second produces one unit per worker. If resources are split evenly between the two firms, average industry productivity per worker will be two units per worker ($(3*100+1*100)/200 = 2$). Assume that 50 workers move to the more productive firm. Average productivity would rise to 2.5 units per worker ($(3*150+1*50)/200=2.5$), a 25 percent productivity boost just by shifting resources between firms. The variance of labor productivity, which describes how widely the productivities are spread, was 1 in the first case; after reallocation it falls to 0.75.[4] Firm size (measured by employment) and productivity are uncorrelated in the first case and positively correlated in the second.

---

4. The sample variance in the first case is $(100*(3-2)^2+100(1-2)^2)/200=1$). After reallocation it is $(150(3-2.5)^2+50(1-2.5)^2=0.75)$.

Alternatively, the growth of relatively unproductive firms can be an indication of public largesse or crony capitalism; the rise of such firms may be immiserating for the country. To see why, imagine that the 50 workers moved from the more productive firm to the less productive firm, perhaps because of government favoritism. In this case productivity would fall and firm size and productivity would become negatively correlated.

Just as large firms are good for growth when they are the most productive but bad for growth when they are relatively weak, the individuals behind them are lauded when they are innovators but criticized when they are cronies. In the United States, the prevailing mythology of the 19th century, when the country was booming, was that large firms grew from small firms by dint of the hard work and perseverance of entrepreneurs or "self-made" men. Indeed, the term "self-made man," attributed to Henry Clay in the 1830s, was used to suggest that the transformation of the United States from an agrarian into a modern commercial economy was a positive development.

The popular aversion to large firms in developing countries—and to some corporations in advanced countries—is related to concerns about political dealing, monopoly power, and/or cronyism. These are all situations where growth stems from special deals given to the firm owners or barriers to entry erected to protect the firm as opposed to the inherent strengths of the firm, and thus productivity and size are unlikely to be positively correlated. Reflecting this view that the dominance of large corporations is not necessarily healthy, a body of literature has grown among economists theoretically exploring the economic costs of cronyism. Anne Krueger (1974) applied the term "rent seeking" to the practice by companies of lobbying for lucrative government licenses and presented evidence of the costs to an economy.[5] More recently firm-level data combined with information about political connections have been used to empirically estimate such costs. But the key intuition is that the capacity for the most productive firms to grow large is critical to economic health.

Evidence on Firm Size

In an efficient and well-managed firm, the most talented and driven employees get promoted; they gain experience and improve their skills, and ultimately earn a spot in a large C-suite office where they have a decision-making role and reap high rewards. Productive and organized workers rise

---

5. Jagdish Bhagwati (1982) describes a broad range of directly unproductive profit-seeking activities that support firms but are costly to the economy.

to middle management, while others perform best specializing in a specific and sometimes limited role in a firm. The workers that repeatedly make mistakes, fail to show up, or cause other costly problems are fired.

Just as workers differ and this leads to various outcomes for employees in a well-run firm, productivities differ and this results in a range of outcomes for firms in a dynamic economy. Some highly productive firms enter, produce the products that are most profitable, reinvest their earnings, and grow. Other firms earn just enough to cover costs and stay in business but have little left over to invest. These firms remain in the market but never grow large. There are also firms that fail to cover costs and these firms exit. Over time, a few very large and highly productive firms account for a disproportionate share of revenues and profits in any given industry.

In fact, a highly skewed firm-size distribution is precisely what is seen across different industries in most countries: a small group of large firms accounts for a very large share of output, exports, and profits. But countries differ in terms of what type of firm rises to the top of the distribution and how large a share of total output the top firms account for.

This section discusses what the firm-size distribution can tell us about the health of the economy.

Larger Shares of Big Firms in Advanced Countries

Firm-size distributions show that the share of resources controlled by large firms tends to increase with the level of development. In the European Union, in higher-income countries like Finland, France, Germany, and the United Kingdom, more than 35 percent of employment in the nonfinancial business sector was in large enterprises (firms with more than 250 employees) in 2010. In contrast, in struggling countries like Italy, Portugal, and Spain, less than 25 percent of employment was in large firms (figure 3.1). (The corresponding share for the United States was 53 percent.)

Large firms account for an even greater share of valued added than employment, implying that they have higher average labor productivity than small firms. Large firms' contribution to value added in Spain and Portugal (34 percent on average) is more than 10 percentage points higher than their contribution to employment, suggesting that if workers moved from small and medium-size firms to large firms, output would increase.

The gap between employment and value added offers information about how much reallocation or labor could improve aggregate productivity. When the gap is large, as in Spain and Portugal, reallocation of labor could greatly boost productivity. In the richer countries of Europe, the

Figure 3.1 Large firms' contribution to employment and value added in Europe, 2010

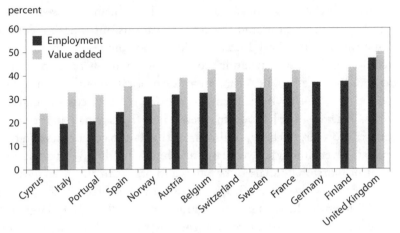

Note: Large firms are firms with more than 250 employees. Data on value added in Germany are not available.

Source: Eurostat, 2010.

gap between employment and value added share is just 3 to 6 percentage points, suggesting that these countries are operating at a higher level of allocative efficiency.

There are problems with this simple approach, as the industries of large and small firms within countries may be very different. The wider gap in Spain and Portugal could be because they specialize in industries that tend to have smaller firms where labor is less productive, but workers from these sectors may not be able to move to the large firms because those sectors require a different set of skills.

But detailed studies of resource allocation across firms within industries find that allocating more resources to the best firms, allowing them to grow large, explains a significant share of the productivity differences across countries. Eric Bartelsman, John Haltiwanger, and Stefano Scarpetta (2013) estimate the covariance between productivity and size in narrowly defined industries in a group of European countries and the United States. They find that allocative efficiency is significantly greater in the United States than in France, Germany, and the United Kingdom. In other words, the most productive US firms absorb a greater share of capital and labor than the most productive European firms. They also find that the covariance between size and productivity was near zero (or negative) at transition in Eastern Europe. Its increase since the early 1990s suggests that allocative efficiency improved sharply in recent decades.

Figure 3.2   Correlation between GDP growth and large firms' share of employment in the United States, 1994–2013

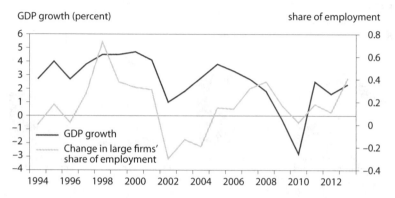

Source: US Bureau of Labor Statistics.

Correlation between GDP Growth and Large Firms' Share of Employment

The United States has a long time series on the share of private sector employment by firm size. Over the past two decades, the employment share of large firms (defined as firms with at least 250 workers) rose from 49 percent to 53 percent.[6] These firms account for a larger share of employment now than in the past, meaning that they accounted for more employment growth than smaller firms.

Large firms in the United States nearly always expand faster than small firms. Figure 3.2 shows the growth in large firms' share of employment and GDP. Both are positive on average, indicating that as the economy gets bigger, large firms attract a larger share of employment. The positive correlation between the two variables (0.49) indicates that large firms absorb more workers during periods of economic growth.

Correlation between Firm Size and Economic Development in Emerging Markets

The World Bank's Enterprise Surveys allow the comparison of firm-size distributions between advanced countries and developing countries. In high-income countries, almost 50 percent of employment is at large firms (defined as firms with more than 100 workers) and 20 percent is at small

---

6. Growth in the importance of large firms is not subject to the definition of firm size: If 1,000 employees is used as the threshold for large firms, their share of employment increased from 36 to 39 percent.

Figure 3.3   Manufacturing firm size distribution in China (2004) and India (2007)

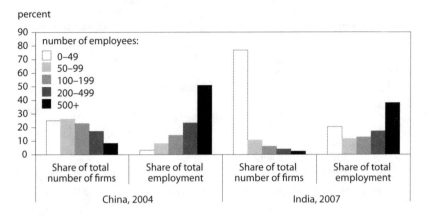

Source: van Ark et al. (2010).

firms (defined as firms with fewer than 20 workers). In contrast, in developing countries 40 percent of employment is in small firms and 30 percent in large firms (IFC 2013). As countries get richer, the share of employment at large firms rises.

The Enterprise Surveys cover only a representative sample. Firm-level data covering the universe of firms have recently become available for a number of developing countries. These data show a highly skewed firm-size distribution in which richer countries have larger firms than poor countries on average. Pedro Bento and Diego Restuccia (2014) use comparable firm-census data for 124 countries with size measured by employment. They show that average firm size increases with the level of development: Every 10 percent increase in per capita income is associated with a 2.6 percent increase in average firm size.

Small firms represent a large share of the total number of firms in an economy but not a large share of employment or value added. In both China and India, the greatest share of manufacturing employment is at large firms (figure 3.3). Such firms account for more than half of manufacturing employment in China, despite accounting for less than 10 percent of firms.

Myth of the Missing Middle

The evidence overwhelmingly suggests that a greater share of large firms is good for growth and development. But until recently many economists considered the problem in developing countries to be the "missing middle"—the absence of a group of mid-sized firms to drive growth and compete with large firms. Indian policymakers were so convinced that small and medium-sized firms drive growth and jobs that in the mid-1970s they restricted 14 percent of the manufacturing sector (about 1,000 products) to small firms. The restrictions remained in place for more than two decades. Indian manufacturing did not thrive during this period, and the restricted sectors missed the boat on global value chains. The firm-size restrictions were removed over a six-year period during the 2000s.

Comparison of the periods with and without size restrictions offers a natural experiment on how small firms perform in the presence and absence of competition from large firms. Leslie Martin, Shanthi Nataraj, and Ann Harrison (2014) find that controlling for other factors of industrial growth, on average removal of the restrictions led to a 7 percent increase in employment, as more productive firms grew. This estimate represents a lower bound, because their research was conducted using data for 2000–07, when adjustment was ongoing. Manuel García-Santana and Josep Pijoan-Mas (2014) estimate that removing the restrictions increased output per worker by roughly 7 percent. The increase in employment coupled with higher labor productivity led to a huge boost in manufacturing growth. Allowing firms to grow large supported both workers and output in India.

Cross-country evidence finds the "missing middle" to be an incorrect characterization of firm distributions in developing countries. Chang-Tai Hsieh and Benjamin Olken (2014) use data from India, Indonesia, and Mexico to underscore that if anything it is large firms that are missing. They find that large firms have higher average productivity and that the fraction of missing firms is increasing in firm size. In other words, there are more missing large firms than missing medium-size firms, one reason why poor countries are poor. Ana Fernandes, Caroline Freund, and Denisse Pierola (2015) find similar results using exporter data and restate the problem as a "truncated top" of the firm-size distribution in developing countries. Exporters tend to be the most productive firms in an economy, so exporter data allow researchers to examine the distribution of a country's good firms. They find that an important reason why developing countries export less is that they are missing the largest superproductive firms—the firm-size distribution is truncated at the top.

Work from a wide variety of developing countries shows similar patterns. Cross-country studies of Africa (Van Biesebroeck 2005), Latin America (Ibarraran, Maffioli, and Stucchi 2009), and the rest of the world (IFC 2013) find that small and medium-size enterprises (SMEs) tend to be less productive than large enterprises and account for a smaller share of productivity growth. A sizable share of the productivity gap between developed and developing countries can be explained by the fact that the estimated share of SMEs in economic activity is 50 percent in developed countries and 70 percent in developing countries. SMEs in developing countries tend to be exceptionally stagnant compared with their developed country peers. Chang-Tai Hsieh and Peter Klenow (2014) estimate that the failure of small firms to grow into large firms reduced productivity growth in manufacturing by 25 percent in Mexico and India compared with the United States.

Big Firms, Fast-Growing Firms, and Job Creation

Small firms are also not big creators of jobs: Rigorous studies based on industrial surveys tend to find that net job growth comes from large firms and startups. The most comprehensive work has been done on the United States, where researchers examine firms as opposed to establishments. Establishment data may lead to size misclassifications. At Walmart, for example, each store may be counted as a medium-size enterprise, but the company is the largest private employer in the world.

Census data include information on entry and exit, which are not observable in subsamples of the universe of firms. Recent work on the United States shows that once firm age is controlled for, most employment creation is by new and young firms and large firms (Haltiwanger, Jarmin, and Miranda 2013). Using census data on Tunisian firms, Bob Rijkers et al. (2014) find similar results: Startups and large firms account for the bulk of net job creation.

Exporting as a Big-Firm Occupation

The skewed distribution of firms is magnified among exporters, among which the top 1 percent of firms account for the lion's share of exports. Large firms account for 80 percent of exports by the United States, more than 50 percent by European countries, and about 50 percent by developing countries. As countries develop, a larger volume of exports tends to come from the largest exporters (figure 3.4). Fernandes, Freund, and Pierola (2015) find evidence that average exporter size grows as countries get richer because allocative efficiency improves: the most productive firms absorb more resources and export more.

Large firms produce and trade on a global stage. They engage in related-party trade (trade between a parent firm and its affiliates), which now accounts for one-third of US exports. Andrew Bernard, Brad Jensen,

Figure 3.4 Correlation between per capita GDP and share of exports by top 1 percent of exporters, 1995–2014

share of exports (percent)

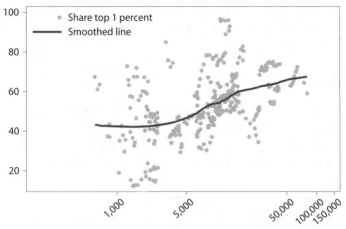

GDP per capita, PPP (constant 2011 international dollars)

PPP = purchasing power parity

Note: Years vary by country.

Sources: Share of exports: World Bank, Exporter Dynamics Database; GDP per capita: World Bank, *World Development Indicators.*

and Peter Schott (2009) show that these globally engaged firms dominate not only trade flows but also employment among trading firms.

A similar pattern emerges in Europe, where exports are concentrated in large firms in the richer and better-performing countries. In France, Germany, and the United Kingdom, large firms account for about 70 percent of total export value. In contrast, in Italy, Portugal, and Spain, such firms account for just 51–56 percent (Cernat, Norman-López, and T-Figueras 2014).

Importance of Individual Firms for Exports

Within the top 1 percent of firms, individual firms explain much export behavior, especially in emerging markets. Using a sample of more than 30 developing countries, Freund and Pierola (2015) show that on average the top firm accounts for 15 percent of a country's exports. The top five firms account for one-third of the value of all exports.

These findings imply that attracting a "superstar" exporter can transform a country's industrial specialization.[7] Sometimes countries attract such a firm through foreign investment (for example, Intel's investment in Costa Rica gave the country a comparative advantage in semiconductors). In other cases, the investment is indigenous (for example, Ahmet Zorlu and his Vestel Group significantly expanded Turkey's television exports). Whatever the source, individuals and their companies can help countries diversify their export basket.

Individuals Matter

Just as the old view was that firms were all the same, the traditional view in the management literature was that individuals did not matter. Capital, labor, and technology mattered; CEOs were regarded as substitutable. Moreover, power was dispersed in large corporations, so no single person mattered.

Anecdotal evidence has always pointed in the other direction. A large and growing body of new research now shows that company leaders matter tremendously. Large private firms create economic growth, but individuals drive firm expansion, especially in the early years of a company's life. When Steve Jobs was forced out of Apple in 1985, the company languished. When he returned more than 10 years later, he reinvented Apple, now the largest technology company in the United States. Warren Buffett is credited with creating a hugely successful conglomerate, despite following a model that is inefficient, according to corporate finance experts. Either Buffett had a unique ability to pick companies or successful companies yearned to be picked by Buffett. Either way a single person made a difference.

Tarun Khanna, Jaeyong Song, and Kyungmook Lee (2011) attribute Samsung's global success to innovations by Lee Kun-Hee, the company's second chair. Lee developed a strategy to ensure that Samsung adopted Western best practices, including merit-based pay and quick promotion for star performers. He brought outsiders into Samsung, required senior Samsung employees to train outside the company, and protected long-term investments in corporate structure and innovation from short-run financial volatility. In a culture where seniority and loyalty are highly valued, these transformational shifts were difficult. An outsider appointed as chief marketing officer for the electronics company is credited with the

---

7. A country is said to have revealed comparative advantage when its export share of a product is greater than the global export share of the product. The intuition is that exporting a larger share of a product than the average country suggests that a country is a relatively efficient producer.

marketing campaign that made the firm a global brand. Samsung staff who spent time abroad and learned foreign languages and cultures are credited with bringing Samsung to places like Thailand and Indonesia. Joint programs with top design institutes, including Parsons in New York, allowed Samsung, once an industry follower, to become a front-runner. Samsung went from being a Korean leader to a global leader under Lee's tenure, with "a brand more valuable than Pepsi, Nike, or American Express," as Khanna, Song, and Lee (2011, 142) note.

Dynamic leaders at emerging-market firms are exhibiting the same traits. As Silicon Valley tycoons focus on smart watches and self-driving cars, China's tech leaders are applying technology to meet Chinese consumers' demands. For example, one of the biggest concerns of consumers is food safety. Tech leaders are developing apps that can scan a product's lifecycle from plant to shelf. Robin Li, of Baidu, is developing smart chopsticks that can test for gutter oil (a major source of illness), ph levels, and calories. Jack Ma ensures that Alibaba adheres to strict rules for pesticides in the products it carries.[8]

Antônio Luiz Seabra of Natura Cosmeticos, the largest cosmetics company in Brazil, was a leader in developing a natural cosmetics line that is environmentally friendly and does not test on animals. His company was ranked second on Corporate Knights' sustainable companies list. He also developed direct marketing to consumers, which had been untried in Brazil, and expanded to other Latin American countries using social networks. Both the product and the customer reach, developed in 1969, were well ahead of their time.

Sam Goi—known in Singapore as the popiah king—moved to Singapore from China when he was six. He dropped out of secondary school after English proved difficult for him. His first attempt at entrepreneurship was a flop. His second company, repairing machines, was a success. But his huge fortune came when he invented a new way to make popiah skins (spring roll wraps). He bought a popiah skin company with 23 people that produced 3,200 skins a day. By mechanizing the process, he turned the company into one that produces 35 million pieces a day, 90 percent of them sold outside Singapore. The company has brought him enormous wealth while bringing consumers throughout Asia lower-cost staples.[9]

---

8. Alexandra Stevenson and Paul Mozur, "China's Long Food Chain Plugs In," *New York Times*, March 2, 2015.

9. "Business Guru," *FT Wealth*, June 2015.

Recent literature on management confirms that a firm's size and value are connected to its leader. Xavier Gabaix and Augustin Landier (2008) find that firm size explains patterns in CEO pay across firms, over time, and between countries. They show that the sixfold increase in CEO pay in the United States between 1980 and 2003 can be fully attributed to the sixfold increase in the market capitalization of large companies during that period.

Using data from the largest 800 US firms for 1969–99, Marianne Bertrand and Antoinette Schoar (2003) find that CEOs explain a large share of the variation in firm policies and outcomes over time, controlling for firm fixed effects and other standard determinants of firm performance. Their results imply that a manager at the 75th percentile invests several times more than a manager at the 25th percentile.

One concern about studies using manager tenure is that the removal of managers when firms perform poorly could drive the results. To get around this problem, Sascha Becker and Hans Hvide (2013) examine entrepreneur death, which is a more exogenous form of leadership change. Using data from Norway they find that entrepreneur death is associated with lower firm growth and higher rates of exit and that the effects are stronger when founders have high levels of human capital.

Using data from Denmark, another study goes a step further to look for an exogenous shock and examines what happens to companies when CEOs *unexpectedly* die (Bennedsen, Pérez-González, and Wolfenzon 2007). The study finds that the death of a CEO leads to on average an 11 percent decline in the operating return on assets. The effects are even stronger in fast-growing industries. Studies of the United States find a high and rising CEO effect, affecting the return on assets and sales by 10 percent in 1950 and 20 percent in the 2000s, and that CEOs matter most at the largest companies.[10] Partly because of CEOs, private companies perform better than state companies. Individuals who build great companies are not easily replaceable, explaining the high rewards they reap.

Prithwiraj Choudhury and Tarun Khanna (2013) evaluate leaders in 42 state-owned research and development (R&D) companies in India. A unique feature of their analysis is that bureaucratic rules, not firm performance, determine leadership turnover. They find that changes in leadership resulted in a 3–15 percent change in the number of patents per government dollar of assistance.

---

10. Walter Frick, "Research: CEOs Matter More Today than Ever, at Least in America," *Harvard Business Review*, March 12, 2014.

Timothy Quigley and Donald Hambrick (2012) take a different tack; they look at what happens when new leaders are more or less constrained to determine whether individual talent and power matter. They explore what happens when a former CEO remains in a leadership position after the appointment of a new CEO. They examine recent CEO successions at 181 high-tech firms. They find that keeping the old CEO on as a board chair restricts the new CEO's power, reducing his or her ability to make changes, such as acquisitions, divestitures, or management restructuring. As a result of these limitations, the likelihood of improved performance is reduced (but the likelihood of worse performance is unaffected). Overall, their results demonstrate that CEO power is one reason why some firms are superstar performers.

Firm leaders are likely to matter even more in emerging markets, where company founders or their descendants tend to run companies. Renée Adams, Heitor Almeida, and Daniel Ferreira (2005) show that when CEOs have more decision-making power, there is significantly more variance in firm performance. Using data on Fortune 500 firms, they find that firms with higher levels of CEO power fall at both ends of the spectrum (best performance and worst performance). They focus on structural power (the power the CEO has over the board and other top executives). They find that having a firm with a CEO founder increases profits by nearly 20 percent.

Flood of New Emerging-Market Mega Firms

The rise of extreme wealth is closely related to the emergence of large firms headquartered in four countries: Brazil, Russia, India, and China. In 1996 these countries were virtually absent from global Fortune 500 or billionaire lists (figure 3.5); in 2014 their wealth and companies captured more than 20 percent of both lists. By 2025 emerging markets are expected to have 45 percent of Fortune 500 companies and 50 percent of the world's billionaires (Dobbs et al. 2013, Knight Frank 2014).

Total revenue from the top five publicly listed firms accounted for 14.6 percent of GDP in Brazil, 20.5 percent in Russia, 15.0 percent in India, and 14.9 percent in China in 2013. This high concentration is not unusual. Even in the United States, which has much deeper markets (with nearly twice as many listed companies and twice the GDP of China in 2013), revenues from the top five listed US companies represented nearly 10 percent of GDP.[11]

Nicholas Lardy of the Peterson Institute for International Economics,

---

11. Company data from Bloomberg and GDP data from the World Bank.

Figure 3.5　Shares of Fortune 500 companies and billionaires in Brazil, Russia, India, and China, 1996–2014

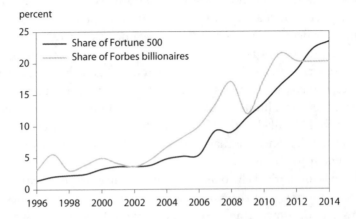

percent

Legend:
— Share of Fortune 500
···· Share of Forbes billionaires

Sources: Data from Fortune 500 and Forbes, The World's Billionaires.

an expert on the Chinese economy, highlights the importance of the private sector in China's growth. While a number of the largest companies in China are state owned, the private sector is rising fast. State enterprises accounted for nearly 80 percent of industrial output in 1978; that share had fallen to just over half by 1990 and to about a quarter by 2011. There were roughly 250 million employees in private firms in urban China in 2011. The growth of employment at these firms accounted for 95 percent of the growth of employment in urban China between 1978 and 2011 (Lardy 2014).

Connecting Firms and Individuals

Figure 3.6 plots the share of Global 2000 companies against the share of billionaires in selected countries in 2014. A point on the 45-degree line indicates the country has the same share of both. Three patterns are clear: (1) Big companies and big money go together, (2) China and the United States have a great deal of both, and (3) some countries are outliers. Brazil and Russia have too much big money given their shares of large corporates, potentially reflecting politically connected money, as opposed to the largely market-made money in other emerging markets. Japan is also an outlier, with relatively little big money given its share of large firms.

China has the lead among emerging markets in its share of large firms, with mainland China alone accounting for 10 percent of firms on the Global 2000 and one-quarter of the FT Emerging Market 500. India comes next, with about half that share.

Figure 3.6 Correlation between share of billionaires and share of big firms, 2014

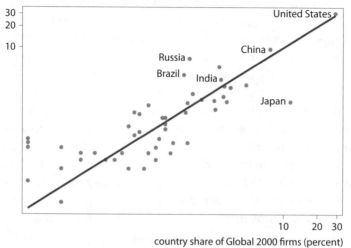

country share of billionaires (percent)

country share of Global 2000 firms (percent)

Sources: Data from Forbes Global 2000 and Forbes, The World's Billionaires.

Firms behind Emerging-Market Growth

The new large companies and their founders have been a constant force behind structural transformation and growth. Brazil, Russia, India, and China together contributed 30 percent of the new fortunes and an even larger share of the new Fortune 500 companies between 1996 and 2014. The four countries accounted for more than 40 percent of real global growth (measured in purchasing power parity, which controls for exchange rate fluctuations) over this period.

Antoine van Agtmael coined the term *emerging market* in 1981 to remove any stigma associated with *third world* in a proposed equity fund to help finance a new group of dynamic corporates (van Agtmael 2007). In his book *The Post-American World*, Fareed Zakaria (2011) talks about the "rise of the rest," referring to the high rates of growth and growing prosperity in Asia and other emerging markets. In *Eclipse: Living in the Shadow of China's Economic Dominance*, Arvind Subramanian (2011) hypothesizes about a future in which China bails the United States out of a financial crisis. The forces behind the phenomenal growth in emerging markets that has captured the attention of these authors are the mega firms and their founders.

Takeaways

The emergence of extreme wealth in emerging markets is a natural part of development and modernization. To the extent that it emanates from mega firms competing in the export sector or other domestic industries with competition and free entry, it is very likely to be progrowth. In general, large private firms and the entrepreneurs behind them help improve resource allocation in a country.

A growing body of literature examines the importance of resource allocation across firms and within industries. It offers support for the importance of highly productive and large firms in development. When resources are drawn to the best firms, a few stars dominate and production grows. Large and more productive businesses come with big rewards, implying that the rise of extreme wealth in emerging markets may be a sign of health—at least to the extent that it is used in competitive industries.

Not only do firms matter, but individuals matter. Extraordinary firm performance is tied to specific leaders and the power they have to make changes at the firm. As a result, high returns accrue to the founders of highly productive large firms, creating a link between wealth and big business.

4

Historical Experiences of Development:
Large Firms and Extreme Wealth

Three big firms—BASF, Bayer, and Hoechst (now Aventis)—established the chemicals industry in Germany at the end of the 19th century, initially specializing in synthetic dyes. Synthetic dyes had just been invented, by the Englishman William Perkin, to serve the large textile industry. Britain was rich in coal, the main input in dye production, and had an early start on the new product. Given the innovation, resources, and market, it should have dominated the market. However, in the 1880s the Germans built large plants that could produce 300 to 400 dyes, compared with the 30 to 40 the British could produce. They also invested in organization and marketing (Bayer, for example, developed a salesforce to work with more than 20,000 customers worldwide). By 1913 two-thirds of the 160,000 tons of dyes produced globally came from these three firms. Similar strategies allowed German companies to dominate pharmaceuticals and other chemicals as well (Chandler 1992, Wegenroth 1997).

The development of the German chemicals industry is the story of a few individuals and their large investments—investments that allowed German firms to control trade in electrical equipment, steel, and office machinery at the expense of smaller British firms. In considering the German experience, as well as the experiences of the United States and other industrial countries, historian Alfred Chandler (1992, 11) writes, "For the past century large managerial enterprises have been engines of economic growth and transformation in modern economies." The same could be written of the recent growth surges in emerging markets.

German industrialists from the period included Werner von Siemens and Johann Georg Halske of Siemens AG, Karl Benz and Gottlieb Daimler of Daimler Benz, Walther Rathenau of AEG, Friedrich Bayer of Bayer Aspirin, Friedrich Engelhorn of BASF, August Thyssen and Friedrich Krupp of Thyssen-Krupp Steel, and Wilhelm von Finck of Allianz. All their companies thrive to this day, and although some fortunes were squeezed during the economic crisis of the 1920s and World War II, many of their descendants remain among Germany's richest people.

The story of the dramatic rise of these industrial titans in Germany illustrates how the Industrial Revolution was inextricably tied to large firms and wealthy industrialists. This chapter examines that history in the United States and Europe and documents similar experiences in the Asian countries that have industrialized more recently. Mega firms and rich industrialists were an essential contributor to the dramatic growth in these economies. Despite their ties to the government, they faced stiff competition in their industrial sectors and emerged on top by dint of factors that went far beyond any favoritism they might have enjoyed. In contrast, attempts to succeed by big firms that were not tied to wealthy individuals have fallen short, as have attempts by countries to grow with wealth but without big firms. An extreme example of the first failure can be found in communism, which experimented with big firms supported by the state but lacking market pressure for the allocation of resources and rewards for the allocation of talent. Communism failed to engender growth because the state directed resources to designated industries and companies rather than to the most efficient or successful firms, while the firms that were successful did not own their profits and hence could not reinvest them. The second failure (wealth without big firms) occurred in a number of other countries when state control or capture of the investment process strangled competition and discouraged innovation and investment. In these instances, wealth accrued not to the owners of the most economically effective firms but to the firms most politically connected. A firm reliant on favoritism within a country may do well domestically, but the record shows that it rarely is able to compete globally.

Big Firms and Big Money during Industrialization

In 1790 Samuel Slater built the first factory in the United States, a textile factory in Rhode Island. By the end of the 19th century, 40 percent of industrial establishments were factories, employing 20 percent of the American workforce. The period of industrialization that followed transformed the country, with the development of industrial centers, factory jobs, and extreme wealth.

The economic development of Indianapolis is a good example of US

**Figure 4.1   Per capita income in BRICS relative to the
United States at similar stages of development**

a. US per capita income, 1840–1929, versus GDP per capita in BRICS, 1996

US GDP per capita, 1990 international dollars

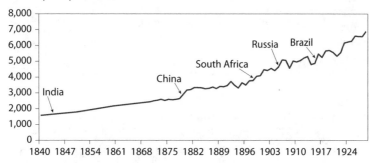

b. GDP per capita in BRICS, 1996–2008

GDP per capita, 1990 international dollars

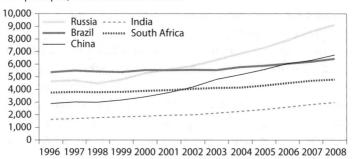

Source: Maddison Project, 2013, www.ggdc.net/maddison/maddison-project/home.htm.

industrialization. In 1850 less than 5 percent of the city's workforce worked in large factories; the share had risen to nearly 60 percent just 30 years later. Factories paid 10 to 25 percent more than small shops, with the largest factories paying the most (Robinson and Briggs 1991). The shift from small-scale production to manufacturing enriched company founders and created the middle-class worker that embodies development.

Emerging markets are at a similar stage of development. Per capita income in the BRICS (Brazil, Russia, India, China, and South Africa) is in the range of that in the United States in 1840–1929 (figure 4.1). Brazil was at the stage of development the United States was during World War I, at the beginning of the period, in 1996; Russia and South Africa were at the level of the United States around the turn of the century; India is at about the level of the United States in 1845; and China is about the level of the United States around 1880. In recent decades growth in the BRICS has

Figure 4.2 Growth in China, 1990–2008, versus growth in the United States, 1890–1908

GDP per capita, 1990 international dollars

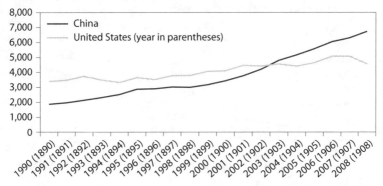

Source: Maddison Project, 2013, www.ggdc.net/maddison/maddison-project/home.htm.

been similar to or more rapid than growth in the United States between 1840 and 1927 (lower panel).

The ease of accessing rich global markets has allowed the BRICS to grow rapidly. Figure 4.2 depicts the growth surge the United States experienced around the turn of the 20th century. It compares changes in US per capita GDP from 1890 to 1908 with China's growth at the turn of the 21st century. China's growth in recent years has been phenomenal even compared with US growth at a similar stage of development. Per capita GDP in China more than tripled over these 18 years—a far larger increase than the 50 percent increase in the United States over a similar period. An important reason why China has grown more rapidly is that lower transportation and trade costs allow large firms to easily access markets both within their borders and abroad, facilitating rapid growth.

Big Business, Big Money during US Industrialization

Industrialization in the United States created extreme wealth. Many household names, such as Andrew Carnegie, John D. Rockefeller, and Cornelius Vanderbilt, grew rich during this time. New technologies and scale economies made large firms many times more competitive than small firms, contributing enormously to productivity growth; falling trade costs allowed these firms to compete globally.

In the tobacco industry, the invention of two machines in the 1880s— one that produced cigarettes and one that packed them—made James B. Duke's American Tobacco company immediately competitive in Europe and Asia, where Imperial Tobacco of Britain had dominated. In food and beverages, high-speed canning and (later) bottling changed production possibilities, leading to the rise of Heinz, Campbell Soup, California Packing (Del Monte), Anheuser-Busch, and Coca-Cola. New machinery to make paper from wood led to the creation of the International Paper Company. Andrew Carnegie combined coke ovens, blast furnaces, and rolling and shaping mills into one massive company that reduced the price of steel from $68 per ton in 1880 to $18 in 1898. John D. Rockefeller's dominance in oil came in the 1870s, when he built the nation's largest refinery, cutting the cost of a gallon of kerosene in half. (Chapter 3 in Chandler, Amatori, and Hikino 1997 discusses these and other examples.)

The increasing concentration of production eventually culminated in the development of antitrust laws, but when these men started their businesses, the industries they were active in were contestable. An important driver of cost saving in steel was competition, not just with US producers but with British firms as well. Rockefeller focused on enhancing productivity to compete internationally. The reduction in cost from building large refineries allowed Standard Oil to undercut Russian and East Indian oil in global markets.

Even services, such as ocean voyages, proved open to entry. The US government heavily subsidized shipping magnate Edward Collins to build steamships that could compete with the British and deliver overseas mail. Cornelius Vanderbilt, who had experience in steamship traffic on the Hudson River, offered to deliver the mail for less. He focused on sturdy, reliable ships and volume, offering innovations such as third-class fares. His improvements and lower costs ultimately forced the Collins (subsidized) line to exit the business (Folsom 1987).

Many of the large companies created in this period—such as General Electric, Exxon and Mobil, Ford, Heinz, Coca-Cola, and US Steel—are still around today. Many of the descendants of the founders remain extremely wealthy.

Robber Barons versus Emerging-Market Tycoons

How do the 28 richest American "robber barons" compare with the 28 richest self-made men of the 1950s and the self-made billionaires in today's emerging markets? Resources account for the largest share in all periods except 2001 (table 4.1). An important difference is the greater significance of tradables and finance among emerging-market billionaires. The higher share of wealth via tradables is a positive indicator for current wealth, since this sector is by definition competitive.

**Table 4.1   Industries of the 28 richest individuals in
the United States and emerging markets**
(percent)

| | United States | | Emerging markets | |
Industry	19th century	1957	2001	2014
Resources	36	50	14	43
Nontradables	32	25	14	7
Finance	21	7	57	29
Tradables and new sectors	11	18	14	21

Sources: Data from Josephson (1934); Lundberg (1968); and Forbes, The World's
Billionaires.

Growth without Large Firms

The mammoth enterprises (businesses with more than 5,000 employees)
that developed in the United States and Germany around the turn of the
century are household names. Similar patterns are evident in Belgium, the
Netherlands, Sweden, and Switzerland.

The smallest European economies were different. Denmark and
Norway had only one or two large firms as other countries were industrializing (Schröter 1997). Denmark had just one large firm, Carlsberg (beer).
Norway had two, Norsk Hydro (fertilizer) and Statoil (oil). Did these economies buck the trend of large firms and rich entrepreneurs? If so, how did
they develop?

Two important features set these countries apart. First, both Denmark
and Norway are very small, with homogeneous populations that numbered
just above 2 million in 1900. Second, both countries have relatively educated
populations and invested in research to make agriculture more efficient.
The early part of their development was connected to feeding Europe; they
were not direct beneficiaries of the industrial movement but gained from
strong demand for agricultural products by their neighbors. The tradition
of open trade that they embraced, which began with agriculture, allowed
them to follow a more standard path in the long run.

Denmark initially specialized in agriculture, especially dairy products.
Its only large firm at the turn of the century was Carlsberg. One explanation for Denmark's success during the industrialization of much of the
rest of Europe is that it benefited from spillovers from trade, climate, and
location. As Europe grew richer, the demand for high-quality animal products rose, and Denmark (and Norway) were there to fill the gap. They had
the right climate and location to export high-quality perishable goods.

Once the structure of agriculture changed and it could no longer employ the Danish population, the superrich and their firms eventually helped the country modernize. Today Denmark has a slightly higher billionaire density given its per capita income than would be predicted based on cross-country data. Danish billionaires are associated with big companies—Lego, Bestseller, JYSK, Coloplast, ECCO—that benefit from international trade (as opposed to finance or resources).

While Norway's development was similar to Denmark's, at least one big company played an important role in its early development. Norway's first large firm, Norsk Hydro, was founded by Sam Hyde, a Norwegian industrialist and engineer, and financed by the Wallenberg family of Sweden, the Swedish version of the Rockefellers. The company developed energy and fertilizer using a revolutionary technique developed by the Norwegian scientist Kristian Birkeland. Norsk Hydro provided the fertilizer that shaped Norway's emergence as an agricultural powerhouse. It remains on the Forbes Global 2000 list to this day, and the Wallenbergs remain one of Sweden's richest families (though most of their $6.4 billion fortune is tied up in foundations). Norway later developed large shipping and oil companies. Today it has the expected density of extreme wealth given its stage of development.

These countries took a somewhat unusual path. Growth was initially fueled by global demand, small-scale agricultural production, and trade. They later took the more traditional path of using large-scale enterprises to modernize.

Big Firms and Big Money in Asia

The United States, Germany, and other European industrializers were not alone in undergoing a transformation toward large firms. Asian economies have witnessed a similar process.

Business and Wealth in Japan

Before World War II, wealth in Japan was dominated by *zaibatsu*—large conglomerates controlled by single families. The four largest were Mitsui (finance and trade), Sumitomo (mining), Mitsubishi (shipping), and Yasuda (banking and insurance). As new industries developed, these business groups expanded. Mitsubishi, for example, moved from shipping into related sectors, including coal, shipbuilding, iron, and marine insurance.

Japanese industrial development was transformed after World War II, when Occupation forces dissolved or reorganized nearly all of the zaibatsu.

The new system of informal business groups (*keiretsu*) maintained a similar structure to the zaibatsu, though ownership was less concentrated. The rise of large private enterprise had already taken hold and continued to thrive. A small number of families retained a significant hold on the economy, although their stakes in the companies were not the majority stakes of the zaibatsu. The keiretsu firms represented just 0.1 percent of all Japanese companies, but their revenues accounted for 25 percent of postwar GDP (Pempel 1998). The biggest change in the shift to the keiretsu was who the rich were: Of the 100 richest people in 1954, not a single one was among the richest in 1944 (Morikawa 1997).

Other Asian Successes

In Korea the *chaebol* (conglomerates) created firms such as Samsung, Hyundai, and Daewoo. In 1973 the top 30 chaebol accounted for less than 10 percent of GDP; by the mid-1980s they held one-third of GDP (Ahn 2010). The families behind industrialization remain in control of the largest firms. Today Samsung's revenue alone is nearly 20 percent of GDP.

Between 1975 and 1990, Korea went from being a poor country with annual per capita income of $3,000 to an upper-middle-income country with per capita income of $8,000 a year (measured in 1990 international dollars). To put this extraordinary growth in context, in 1975 income in South Korea was about equal to income in Nicaragua; the country was sandwiched between North Korea and Namibia in terms of level of development. Despite few natural resources, by 1990 South Korea ranked in the top third of countries. In 1975 per capita income was just 19 percent of US per capita income; by 1990 it had risen to 38 percent, and in 2008 it was over 60 percent.

Singapore grew thanks to a combination of domestic and foreign investment. Now one of the richest countries in the world, at independence in 1965 the tiny island of 3 million people had a real per capita income that was barely above that of Guatemala and lower than that of Jamaica. Just seven years later, one-quarter of Singapore's manufacturing firms were either foreign owned or joint ventures.

The importance of foreign investment in Singapore's takeoff separates it from the national industrialists of Germany, the United States, and Japan. Foreign multinationals have the expertise and capital to build large, efficient plants almost overnight, transforming a country's productivity frontier. In Singapore large foreign multinationals built a domestic industry that supported rapid investment. The excellent business climate fostered by its founder, Lee Kuan Yew, who encouraged foreign investment and promoted education and infrastructure improvements (while limiting civil liberties), allowed a small country with no natural resources except its location to grow economically at one of the fastest rates in history. Its probusiness climate encouraged one large company after another to choose Singapore as a hub.

Foreign investment generated a new dynamic in which domestic business investment was drawn to complementary industries that required local knowledge. This combination of foreign and domestic enterprises supported the growth of commerce, building the logistics industry that made Singapore so attractive as a business destination.

Chang Yun Chung, for example, cofounded Pacific International Lines in 1967, after Singapore split from Malaysia. The company is now one of the largest shipping companies in the world, with a fleet of 180 ships. Another shipping magnate, Lim Oon Kuin, began by delivering diesel fuel to fishermen. From there he moved into shipping and logistics.

Today the density of the superrich in Singapore is among the highest in the world. As in other countries, extreme wealth in Singapore came with growth.

China's Mega Firms

Development in China is following a pattern similar to that of earlier modernizers. In 2014 China was home to the world's 3 largest public companies and 5 of the top 10.[1] As elsewhere, development in China has come with large firms and large fortunes.

Table 4.2 shows the number of top 500 largest firms by country. The big gainers from 1962 to 1993 were Japan and Korea, at the expense of the United States and the United Kingdom. From 1993 to 2014, China and Russia were the main gainers, at the expense of Japan and the United States.

Table 4.2 shows an extraordinary gain in the number of mega firms in China from 1993–2014, similar to the expansion in Japan from 1962 to 1993. Chong-En Bai, Chang-Tai Hsieh, and Zheng Song (2014) examine why large firms and the individuals behind them have supported development in China, despite what in the West might be considered cronyism or state capitalism. They argue that local governments, which hand out favors, compete with one another, effectively putting incentives in the right

---

1. Liyan Chen, "The World's Largest Companies: China Takes over the Top Three Spots," *Forbes*, May 7, 2014.

Table 4.2 Number of top 500 largest firms, by country, 1962, 1993, and 2014

Economy	1962	1993	2014	Economy	1962	1993	2014
Advanced economies				**Emerging markets**			
United States	298	160	128	China	0	2	95
Japan	31	135	57	India	1	5	8
France	27	26	31	Russia	0	0	8
Germany	36	32	28	Brazil	0	2	7
United Kingdom	55	43	27	Taiwan	0	2	5
South Korea	0	11	17	Mexico	1	3	3
Switzerland	6	9	13	Indonesia	0	0	2
The Netherlands	5	9	12	Singapore	0	0	2
Canada	13	7	10	Turkey	0	3	1
Italy	7	7	9	South Africa	2	4	0
Australia	2	10	8	Other emerging markets	0	0	9
Spain	0	3	8	Total emerging markets	4	21	140
Sweden	8	12	3				
Ireland	0	0	2				
Belgium	3	4	2				
Norway	0	3	1				
Finland	0	3	1				
Austria	1	2	1				
Other advanced economies	0	3	2				
Total of both advanced economies and emerging markets					496	500	500

Note: For 1962 and 1993, the top 500 companies are ranked by sales. For 2014 companies are ranked based on additional metrics. See the 2014 Fortune 500 list for explanation of the methodology used in 2014.

Sources: Data for 1962 and 1993: Chandler, Amatori, and Hikino (1997); data for 2014: Fortune 500 list.

place. One example they give is the East Hope Group, owned by billionaire Liu Yongxing. The group expanded from agribusiness to aluminum with help from the local government of Sanmenxia, a city in Henan Province with large bauxite deposits. A state-owned firm had the exclusive right to purchase bauxite, but the Hope Group managed to negotiate a deal with local officials to obtain bauxite, despite resistance from the incumbent monopoly. Hope began producing aluminum in 2005, and other private firms followed; by 2008 the market share of the state-owned firm had fallen to 50 percent. Ultimately, the market proved contestable, open to entry.

In the automotive sector, competition developed between Shanghai-GM and Chery (a company based in the city of Wuhu). Working through local government officials, Chery eventually managed to get a license from the central government to make cars for the province, which then turned into a license to sell throughout China. The company is now one of the largest car producers in China. "Competition between local governments may have played a central role in allowing new firms to emerge and challenge incumbent firms. This is important for technical progress and long-run growth," according to Bai, Hsieh, and Song (2014, 7).

China is a large enough country that competition can come from within, as municipalities compete. Most developing-country firms, however, require the push and pull of global markets to grow. The push from openness provides incentives to innovate and use resources efficiently. A car producer capable of competing with European and American firms, as the Japanese and later Korean firms did, must use new technologies. Foreign markets offer a much bigger market, which facilitates rapid growth. For these companies the incentive to grow large comes from the prospect of tapping global markets that are accessible if a firm is good enough.

Contested versus Uncontested Wealth

In many cases money and large firms do not go beyond borders, as happened with the Ben Ali–connected firms in Tunisia or the Marcos-connected firms in the Philippines. These firms are less likely to produce the type of wealth that lands owners on the Forbes World's Billionaires List. The experiences of the United States, Japan, South Korea, and China show that big business, even with some cronyism, still promotes economic growth, provided markets are contestable. The main constraint to growth through big business is when the firms compete in protected domestic markets.

Argentina during the turn of the 19th century is an example of a country that appeared ready to take off. With real per capita income similar to France and between Sweden and Germany, an influx of foreign investment, and labor, Argentina was primed to grow. But the boost from railways and transportation that allowed the United States to become a manufacturing center never materialized in Argentina. One explanation is that import-substitution policies incentivized business to focus on supplying the small Argentine market. Inward-looking policies delayed industrialization because the market was too small for firms to benefit from returns to scale and the lack of competition meant that there was less competitive pressure on resource allocation. As a result, the industrial development of Argentina remained incomplete, and as of 1929 the largest firms remained in food, tobacco, and some textiles but little manufacturing (Barbero 1997).

The importance of competition cannot be overstated. To see how the orientation, size, and global reach of the firms associated with extreme wealth matters, it is informative to compare Chile and Tunisia, two small middle-income countries with populations of less than 20 million. In 1985 the two countries were at a similar stage of development, with per capita income of $1,000 to $1,500. In 2014 the average Chilean, with a per capita income of $15,230, was more than three times as rich as the average Tunisian.[2] Chile had a dozen billionaires in 2014; Tunisia had none.

Horst Paulmann, the second-richest person in Chile, founded Cencosud, one of Latin America's biggest retail chains. He opened the first hypermarket (more than 5,000 square feet) in 1976, moving into Argentina in the 1980s as the company pioneered retail globalization in the region. Cencosud is now the fourth-largest grocery chain in Latin America. It owns 645 supermarkets in Argentina, Brazil, Chile, and Peru and competes with global companies like Walmart and Carrefour, as well as other Latin American chains. The company controls 11 percent of the Chilean grocery market.[3]

The largest Tunisian retail chains operate under licenses from French chains. The largest, Casino, is owned by Marouane Mabrouk, who is married to the youngest daughter of former president Zine El Abidine Ben Ali.[4] The second-largest, Carrefour, is owned by the Ulysse Trading and Industrial Companies (UTIC), the conglomerate by Taoufik Chaibi, whose nephew is married to Ben Ali's second daughter. Together these companies control two-thirds of the Tunisian market. These franchises enriched their owners, but they failed to create innovative businesses that spread globally or create billions in wealth for their owners.

What the Tunisian experience highlights is that the emergence of large firms is critical for growth but not sufficient. Three ingredients are needed: entrepreneurs, mega firms, and competition. Government connections are not necessarily detrimental to growth, as long as firms are forced to compete globally. Bob Rijkers, Caroline Freund, and Antonio Nucifora (2014) show that President Ben Ali and his extended family controlled a large share of Tunisia's private sector—so much so that 21 percent of all corporate profits accrued to them.[5] The family was most prominent in nontradable sectors,

---

2. Calculated using gross national income per capita in current US dollars.

3. "Top Grocery Retailers in Latin America," *Agriculture and Agrifood Canada*, August, 2012.

4. "Corruption in Tunisia Part III: Political Implications," *WikiLeaks*, October 12, 2011.

5. Ishac Diwan, Philip Keefer, and Marc Schiffbauer (2014) find similar results in Egypt for Mubarak cronies before the 2011 revolution.

such as telecommunications, transportation, retail, and hotels, where they benefited from monopoly power and used the regulatory environment to reap profits. Instead of creating a business-friendly climate in Tunisia, they used the investment code as a get-rich-quick tool to protect their domestic interests. Ben Ali signed decrees limiting domestic and foreign entry into sectors where family firms were prominent. One example is the failed entry of McDonald's into Tunisia. The company was reportedly refused access when it rebuffed a request from Ben Ali's family members for the lucrative franchise and instead requested competitive bidding. This type of concentration in large domestically oriented firms with little competition from foreign direct investment reduces competition. Firms in such markets lack the incentive and innovation necessary to compete in global markets. They become large in domestic markets, not globally competitive.

In the late 1990s, similar problems of uncompetitive crony capitalism arose in some East Asian countries, where corporate wealth was concentrated in the hands of a few families, to the detriment of development (Claessens, Djankov, and Lang 2000). About 17 percent of the total value of listed corporate assets in Indonesia and the Philippines was controlled by a single family (the Suharto family in Indonesia, the Marcos family in the Philippines), with 10 families controlling half of all corporate assets in each country. The Suharto family controlled 417 listed and unlisted companies, through business groups led by children, other relatives, and business partners, many of whom also held or had held government offices. Imelda Marcos, the widow of former Philippine president Ferdinand Marcos, described her family's economic power as follows: "We practically own everything in the Philippines, from electricity, telecommunications, airlines, banking, beer and tobacco, newspaper publishing, television stations, shipping, oil and mining, hotels and beach resorts down to coconut milling, small farms, real estate, and insurance."[6] Like the Ben Ali clan, the Marcos family focused on domestically consumed sectors, a clear indication that wealth was not being created in contestable markets.

Big Firms without Wealth Creation

In Argentina, Tunisia, the Philippines, and Indonesia, wealth was created without globally competitive firms. At the opposite extreme was the Soviet Union, which created mega firms without wealth.

For a brief period, when the best firms were nationalized, the system

---

6. Tony Tassel, "Mrs. Marcos in Legal Fight to Get $13bn," *Financial Times*, December 8, 1998.

seemed to work. State trusts were created from the most successful of the nationalized companies in the early 1920s. At first firms performed well, as the least productive factories were shuttered. The problem was that only 20 percent of the profits of each trust were retained as reserve capital; 80 percent was remitted to the state budget, constraining growth by the best-performing firms. From the 1920s to the 1970s, centralized investment as a share of total investment increased from 45 to 71 percent. The best companies were not allowed to thrive, as there was neither incentive nor ability to expand production (Yudanov 1997). The worst companies were not closed but subsidized by the better companies.

The state-owned behemoths did not grow through the same process as the emerging-market giants. Rather than flowing to the most productive firms, capital and labor were simply directed to certain firms. This allocation of resources did not create wealth or spur growth.

Effects of Wealth on the Economy

The theme of this book is that development depends on big business and a competitive environment, one outcome of which is the creation of enormous personal fortunes. A problem is that competition can get hijacked along the way by the power money creates, stalling the process. Once created, a powerful business class will seek to protect its interests. To the extent that doing so involves erecting barriers to entry or eliciting subsidies, consumers will suffer; to the extent that it involves protecting property rights or promoting democracy, citizens will benefit.

Restriction of Competition

Once large firms and fortunes are created, company founders may seek government interventions to maintain market share or growth. When the national champions are large exporters, global competition naturally tames the most egregious demands. In countries where the biggest firms compete on global markets, foreign competition limits the effectiveness of the most costly government policies. For example, restricting trade or creating domestic entry barriers are costly because they reduce competition and raise consumer prices, but these policies are ineffective in promoting a large exporting firm that competes with foreign firms on the global market. The policies sought by the business community are most welfare reducing when the main market of the largest firms is the domestic one. The concern about preserving competition once large companies are created is therefore especially relevant in large economies like the BRICS, where many firms are primarily dependent on local consumers and may therefore benefit from barriers to entry.

One such example can be found in the Chinese insurance sector, where not surprisingly the customer base is domestic. Close government and business relations in China allowed Ping An Insurance to protect its monopoly power, enriching a political leader and his family. After the Asian financial crisis, large financial companies in China were broken up, in a process overseen by Wen Jiabao, China's vice premier at the time. Ping An Insurance resisted, "humbly requesting that the vice premier lead and coordinate the matter from a higher level."[7] The company remained intact and is now one of China's largest financial services company, bigger than AIG, Metlife, or Prudential. The Wen family is estimated to have made more than $2 billion on its shares in Ping An as of 2007.[8]

In the United States, the robber barons also attempted to maintain monopoly power, but the government ultimately stepped in. The Chinese government is similarly responding. China's antimonopoly law, adopted in 2007, was long in the making. Pressure from foreign governments, accession to the World Trade Organization, and the Chinese reform agenda have all been credited with its development. External observers have found the new law to be compatible with laws in the West and note that it is being enforced (Mariniello 2013). The main concern about Chinese competition policy is that it will be used aggressively against foreign firms operating in China, not that it will fail to discipline Chinese monopoly power, which unfortunately will also limit competition.

The process of private businesses in China growing large, misbehaving, and eventually being regulated is not very different from developments in the United States during the late 19th century. In order to control markets, large firms in industries like railroad and oil colluded on prices or quantities, but firms always attempted to cheat to corner the market. One way around this problem was to create trusts, conglomerates that had large stakes in all of the leading firms in the same industry. Trusts effectively ruled the market, stopping entry of new unconnected firms and setting prices.

Consumers in the United States were outraged, as the media reported price increases on a number of commodities. Congress took action in 1890, passing the Sherman Antitrust Act. The law took many years to be implemented, but it remains in use as an important tool to prevent anti-

---

7. David Barbosa, "Lobbying, a Windfall and a Leader's Family," *New York Times*, November 24, 2012.

8. Ibid.

competitive behavior. In large countries, and in sectors that are inherently noncompetitive, creating and implementing competition law becomes increasingly important as countries develop.

Protection of Property Rights

Attempts by business to protect their interests are not always bad for the economy. The desire to safeguard wealth can lead to better protection of property rights and better polity, because a powerful state always has means to expropriate.

In the Middle Ages, a new class of large-scale industrialists promoted institutional reform by demanding property rights and legal protection. Daron Acemoglu, Simon Johnson, and James Robinson (2005) show that between 1500 and 1800, the European countries that traded most with the New World grew fastest and that when institutions were adaptable, the trading countries had the most rapid institutional development and growth. They argue that Atlantic trade created a powerful commercial class, which demanded property rights to protect its business interests. As long as there were significant checks on the monarchy, institutions adapted. They compare England and the Netherlands, where commercial interests developed outside of the Crown and pressed for protection of their businesses, with Portugal and Spain, where they did not.

Supporting this view, Saumitra Jha (2015) uses detailed data on the assets of members of England's parliaments in 1628 and 1640–60. He finds that moderates who held shares in major companies abroad were more likely to support revolutionary reforms. Jha argues that the economic opportunity created by overseas investment was critical in consolidating the parliamentary majority for reform. Business interests and openness to trade and investment played an important role in institutional development.

Influence over the Political System

How the rich are likely to influence politics in emerging markets remains unclear. The rich may have different political preferences from the rest of the population and succeed in effecting change that is bad for the majority. But they may also act in the interests of the people. In autocracies, for example, the preferences of the new rich may be closer to those of the population than to the leadership.

While the issue of the excessive political influence of businesspeople is beyond the scope of this book, one common theme that emerges from the literature on the subject is that the rich use their money and influence to get their interests served by government, often at the expense of the rest of the population.[9] Much of the literature focuses on the United States, where campaign stops at the summer homes of the rich are a national pastime and wealth seems to be playing a bigger and bigger role in government.

In contrast, in emerging markets, many of which are not well-established democracies, elites may help rein in a powerful leader. The superrich sometimes take extreme risks to promote democracy (examples include Mikhail Khodorkovsky of Russia and Wang Gongquan of China, both of whom spent time in prison and lost their fortunes). Before billionaires from China dominated the list of the richest people from emerging markets, the conventional wisdom was that the government prevented any one person from getting too rich because the associated power might threaten the government's control. It remains to be seen in which, if any, direction Jack Ma, Robin Li, or Ma Huateng will push the Chinese government.

US history is, of course, not absent elites who did great things. George Washington, Thomas Jefferson, James Madison, and James Monroe were all part of the slave-owning planter aristocracy when they started the revolution. Madison wrote the Constitution.

Indeed, a body of literature shows that it is the elites who tend to promote political change. Connections to government officials are useful. But given that other wealthy people can exploit their connections (to the detriment of competitors), the wealthy class may prefer rules and accountability. Alessandro Lizzeri and Nicola Persico (2004) argue that British elites favored democracy (broader franchise) precisely because it offered better incentives to politicians—less pork-barrel politics.

Since Seymour Lipset (1959), a large body of literature has found a strong link between economic development and democracy. It is hard therefore to argue that large-scale private business, which has been an integral part of successful development, is inimical to democracy. South Korea de-

---

9. Darrell West (2014) finds that billionaires have sought public office in 13 countries, 7 of them emerging markets (India, Georgia, Lebanon, the Philippines, Russia, Thailand, and Ukraine). Once in office, they pursue policies that are very specific to their interests. The most striking example is Georgia's Boris Ivanishvili, who, having made his fortune in Russia, made it his mission to eliminate the anti-Russian sentiment that was prevalent in the previous regime. West discusses the behind-the-scenes influence of the superrich in detail, with a focus on the United States and campaign contributions. John Kampfner (2014) notes that the elite of 2,000 years ago are similar to today's superrich, some of whom are hypercompetitive, paranoid, and consumed with the desire to be remembered. As a result, they tend to interfere in politics. Kevin Phillips (2002) shows how the rich have worked with the politically powerful throughout US history, supporting their joint interests.

veloped the chaebol first and democracy later. Carlos Slim bought Telmex from the government before Mexico democratized. In Eastern Europe big business and democracy have for the most part grown up together. Evelyne Huber, Dietrich Rueschemeyer, and John Stephens (1993), who examine democratization in the advanced countries and Latin America, argue that economic development promotes democracy precisely because of the growing capitalist class. Capitalist transformation is important because it enlarges the working and middle classes and facilitates self-organization. The transition from a landed upper class to an industrial upper class with a thriving middle class and urbanization promotes a democratic shift. Huber, Rueschemeyer, and Stephens interpret the data to mean that an agricultural elite is in general bad for democracy; big business is not. From this perspective, it is not surprising that the Middle East and North Africa, the least democratized region in the world, is also the least globally integrated region and one in which big business is least developed.

The political ramifications of growing wealth in emerging markets are worth watching, and they will not all be negative. The rise of company founders competing in global markets is a positive sign, because they are likely to be more connected to citizens and global values than to specific government officials, especially compared with billionaires associated with resource-related or inherited wealth.

Takeaways

The vast majority of countries never experience high rates of growth for a long enough stretch of time to become rich. The few that have accomplished this feat in the past two centuries did so with the help of private ownership, large firms, and competition. Crony capitalist systems have created big business, wealth, and growth only when the largest firms compete in global markets.

Big money, big business, competition, and development all work together. Highly concentrated wealth without globally competitive large firms (as in Tunisia) has not led to growth, and large firms that did not create wealth (as in the Soviet Union) did not spur development.

5

Big Business, Structural Transformation, and Development

Every year the biggest companies in emerging markets employ more and more people. Mexico's largest private employer is Walmex, with nearly 250,000 employees. The company was founded as Cifra by Jerónimo Arango in 1952 and acquired by Walmart in the 1990s. Arango is now worth $4.6 billion. Mexico's second-largest private employer is Femsa, the leading beverage company in Latin America, with over 200,000 workers, owned by billionaires Eva Gonda Rivera and José and Francisco Calderón Rojas. Other members of the superrich founded companies like BRF in Brazil, Cencosud in Chile, and Midea in China, all of which employ more than 100,000 workers each.

The Financial Times (FT) Emerging Market 500 list reflects this trend. In 2011, when the list was launched, 16 million people worked at the top 500 largest emerging-market companies. By 2014 the figure had risen to 19 million. The number of employees per firm on the FT Global 500 has risen in each of the BRIC (Brazil, Russia, India, and China) economies (figure 5.1).

This chapter examines how these superentrepreneurs and their mega firms contribute to the process of structural transformation. It shows that these large-scale employers move workers out of agriculture and into more productive jobs in factories and retail, which offer higher pay and a path to a different life. This force is unique in the emerging markets because these economies are still industrializing. In contrast, in advanced countries structural transformation is at a later stage, with workers moving out of industry into services.

This positive effect of mega firms on employment contrasts sharply with the often-reported deplorable working conditions in large develop-

Figure 5.1 Average employment per FT Global 500 firm in the BRIC countries, 2009–14

employees per firm, thousands

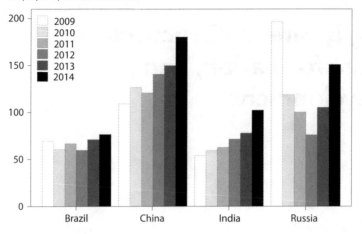

Source: Data from FT Global 500.

ing-country factories. For example, the 14 suicides at Foxconn in China and the fire at the Tazreen Fashion factory in Bangladesh, which killed more than 100 people, are appalling. But it is also true that the millions of workers who leave more difficult rural lives are able to earn more working in factories, thus taking their first steps out of poverty.

Leslie Chang, a *Wall Street Journal* reporter who lived in China for 10 years, writes about employment opportunities from the workers' perspectives in her book *Factory Girls: From Village to City in a Changing China.* She followed two migrant workers in Dongguan, a factory city in South China, for three years. She found that although the work was hard, the women were optimistic, because the factories offered them social mobility—the potential for a better life with many more options than their rural villages offered. Returning with one of the women to her home village, she discovers the poverty and boredom that spurred their departure.

Despite some hiccups, mega firms have increased living standards and growth in most emerging markets. Factory jobs are better than subsistence farming, and they offer the potential for mobility for those able to train for such work. Mega firms and the innovative entrepreneurs behind them are a necessary part of the path to modernization, because they are a large and immediate source of jobs. The early stage of development is contingent on the presence of globally competitive firms and moving people out of agriculture and into industry.

Projected Increases in Extreme Wealth in Emerging Markets

The number of extremely wealthy individuals in emerging markets is rising rapidly. By 2023 the share of billionaires in emerging markets will equal or exceed the share in advanced countries, and about one-third of the people worth $100 million or more will live in emerging markets (table 5.1).

Table 5.1 Emerging-market share of world's wealthiest people, 2003, 2013, and 2023 (percent of total)

| | | | 2023 | |
Level of wealth	2003	2013	Knight Frank estimates	Author's estimate based on recent historical growth rates in emerging markets
Ultra-high-net-worth individuals (people worth $30 million or more)	13	22	26	27
Centimillionaires (people worth $100 million or more)	14	25	31	33
Billionaires	26	43	50	52

Source: Author's estimates using data from Knight Frank.

Extreme Wealth and Structural Transformation

Unlike some advanced countries, where median incomes have stagnated and the employed share of the population has declined, manufacturing employment and wages in China have been rising rapidly. The US Bureau of Labor Statistics estimates that from 2002 to 2009, 13 million people entered manufacturing in China (nearly the size of the US workforce in manufacturing) (Banister 2013). Over this period, average manufacturing wages nearly tripled.

This type of rapid structural transformation—the move out of agriculture and into industry—is a standard feature of development. Margaret McMillan, Dani Rodrik, and Inigo Verduzco-Gallo (2014) show that Asia's recent growth has been stronger than Latin America's and Africa's mainly because of the structural change that moved employment into the most productive manufacturing industries in Asia, but which failed to materialize in the other regions. Figure 5.2 documents the relationship between GDP per capita and the number of billionaires per 100 million people and the sectoral composition of employment. As countries develop, the number of billionaires rises (top panel). The structural transformation

Figure 5.2 Correlation between extreme wealth and structural transformation, 1996–2014

billionaires per 100 million people, log scale

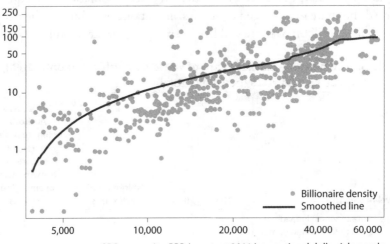

GDP per capita, PPP (constant 2011 international dollars), log scale

employment share

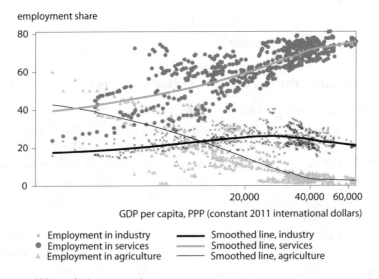

GDP per capita, PPP (constant 2011 international dollars)

× Employment in industry ——— Smoothed line, industry
● Employment in services ——— Smoothed line, services
▲ Employment in agriculture ——— Smoothed line, agriculture

PPP = purchasing power parity

Sources: Data from World Bank, *World Development Indicators*; and Forbes, The World's Billionaires.

that accompanies the development process coincides with the movement of labor from the agricultural sector into manufacturing and services (bottom panel). As countries develop, the share of labor in agriculture declines and service employment increases, especially in the later stage of development. The share of employment in industry rises until per capita income reaches about $25,000 (in constant 2011 international dollars) and then declines.

An important question is whether large-scale entrepreneurship and the extreme wealth that comes with it hasten structural transformation or are merely outcomes of structural transformation and growth. Put differently, controlling for stage of development, is the presence of a higher density of extreme wealth associated with more rapid structural transformation?

One way to answer this question is to examine the correlation between wealth and structural transformation, controlling for country-specific characteristics and the stage of development. Even controlling for country-specific factors that do not change over time, such as geography and relative size, and controlling for per capita income, countries that create more billionaires also move more rapidly to the next stage of development—from agriculture to industry in the South and from industry to services in the North (figure 5.3).[1]

Holding country-specific factors and income growth constant, agricultural employment in an emerging-market country where the number of billionaires rises from two to four would be expected to decrease by nearly 2 percentage points more than in a country that did not witness the same expansion in extreme wealth. The results shown in figure 5.3 are consistent with the notion that billionaires and their mega firms accelerate structural transformation at early stages of development.

Self-Made Founders Employ the Most People

How many workers are directly employed by the rich? Of the firms on the 2014 FT Emerging Market 500 list, 109 are connected to one or more billionaires. Table 5.2 shows the average number of employees according to the type of billionaire connected to these companies. Company founders employ the largest number of people, with an average of 80,000 employees in the companies they started. Given that by definition their firms are new firms, all of these jobs are new ones (job creation).

Compared with small business (table 5.2, column 4), billionaire firms perform well in terms of job creation. The total direct employment from this select group of firms remains small, however: The nearly 700 emerging-market billionaires employ about 44 million people or just over 1 percent of the 4 billion people of working age in emerging markets. Considering that the big firms are not meant to employ all of a country's workers but to enhance the

---

1. The results are highly significant despite the fact that industrialization has gotten more difficult since 1990 as a result of labor-saving technologies and globalization (Rodrik 2015).

Figure 5.3 Correlation between extreme wealth and employment by sector in advanced countries and emerging economies, 1996–2014

partial correlation

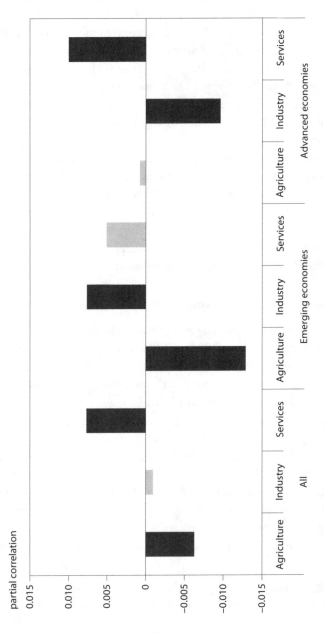

Note: Bars report the coefficients on the log of the number of billionaires from the regression of the share of employment by sector on the log of billionaires, country fixed effects, and the log of GDP per capita. Dark gray bars indicate significance at the 1 to 5 percent level.

Source: Author's calculations.

Table 5.2   Employment by emerging-market billionaires, 2014

Type of billionaire	Number of billionaires	Share of emerging-market billionaires (percent)	Average number of employees	Number of businesses with 50 employees needed to employ same number of employees
Executive	16	11.8	47,387	948
Company founder, nonfinance	42	30.9	79, 291	1,586
Privatization and resource-related	22	16.2	75,725	1,515
Self-made finance	17	12.5	56,435	1,128
Inherited wealth	39	28.7	57,511	1,150
Total	136	100.0	62,752	1,255

Note: Figures are based on billionaires associated with FT Emerging Market 500 firms, a list that excludes Israel and Hong Kong. Small businesses are companies with fewer than 50 employees.

Sources: Data from the FT Emerging Market 500 and Forbes, The World's Billionaires.

pull out of agriculture, the numbers are a bit higher. In China, for example, about 320 million people work in agriculture. If each billionaire employed 63,000 people (the average in table 5.2), China's 151 newly minted billionaires would have absorbed about 10 million workers from 2002 to 2014, only about 3 percent of the agricultural sector, but a substantial number compared with the 13 million workers who, the US Bureau of Labor Statistics estimates, moved into manufacturing from 2002 to 2009 (Banister 2013).

These direct calculations may understate the importance of big business in structural transformation for several reasons. First, billionaires are the focus of this book because their businesses are identifiable and a long cross-country time series is available on them. But their presence is meant to capture more broadly the big business environment and the type of businesspeople (origins and sectors) a country is developing. In reality, many large-scale entrepreneurs, not just billionaires, bring about structural transformation. The cross-sectional correlation between the populations of centimillionaires and billionaires is very high for the years available (0.95), implying that the effect of the superrich could be picking up this broader group, which employs a much larger share of the workforce.

Second, these direct job numbers underestimate the value of each business, because they ignore spillover effects on upstream and downstream industries. For example, makers of pharmaceuticals purchase chemicals and machinery to produce their products and use logistics and retail outlets to get their products to market. The estimates also ignore income effects, as employees spend money on consumer goods.

Third, the superrich have many additional businesses other than their main source of wealth, which are not included in these calculations. For example, Robin Li, founder of Chinese internet company Baidu, which employed 46,000 people in 2014, has ownership stakes in 51 companies, which together employ an additional 33,000 people.

Emerging-Market Firms Displace Advanced-Country Firms

Emerging-market companies are growing rapidly, overtaking advanced-country firms at the top of the Forbes Global 2000 list. As recently as 2009, all 10 of the world's largest firms were advanced-country firms. In 2010 the Chinese bank ICBC became the first emerging-market company to be part of the top 10; by 2014 Chinese banks captured the top three places on the Global 2000 list, with a fourth Chinese bank taking the number 10 spot.

Figure 5.4 shows the change in the number of advanced-country and emerging-market mega firms between 2006 and 2014 by sector. Most industries fall in the bottom right-hand quadrant, where firms are entering from the South and exiting from the North. In banking, for example, 61 emerging-market firms joined the list between 2006 and 2014 and 77 advanced-country firms exited.

In others sectors the growth of mega firms in the North and the South is more even, with both groups showing rising shares. These sectors (shown in the upper-right-hand quadrant) include household goods, oil, and capital goods. Growing emerging-market demand helps explain these booming global sectors. As the number of consumers in the world grows and they get richer, demand for household goods rises. The infrastructure investment needed for structural transformation also boosts global demand for capital goods and oil.

The South has seen big gains in materials producers, such as Jiangxi Copper (China) and Magnitogorsk Iron and Steel (Russia). This shift is also related to structural transformation. As emerging markets play a bigger role in the global economy, there is more demand for raw materials, such as steel and coal, to build industry.

Business school professors, investors, and consulting companies are closely watching these emerging-market mega firms. Studies of their extraordinary growth have incited fears that they will steal consumers from established advanced-country firms. Typical titles include *Emerging Markets Rule: Growth Strategies of the New Global Giants* (Guillén and García-Canal 2013), *The Emerging Markets Century: How a New Breed of World Class Companies Is Overtaking the World* (van Agtmael 2007), and *The Rise of the Emerging-Market Multinational* (Accenture 2008).

Figure 5.4 Replacement of mega firms from advanced countries by mega firms from emerging markets, by sector, 2006–14

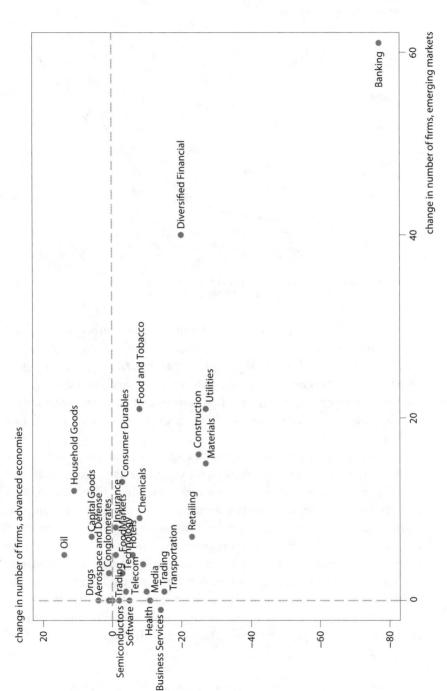

change in number of firms, advanced economies

change in number of firms, emerging markets

Oil
Household Goods
Capital Goods
Drugs
Aerospace and Defense
Conglomerates
Consumer Durables
Insurance
Trading
Tech
Food
Markets
Telecom
Hotels
Chemicals
Semiconductors
Software
Health
Media
Trading
Business Services
Transportation
Retailing
Food and Tobacco
Construction
Materials
Utilities
Diversified Financial
Banking

Source: Data from Forbes Global 2000, 2006 and 2014.

95

**Figure 5.5   Stock of outward foreign direct investment by
developing and developed economies, 1981–2013**

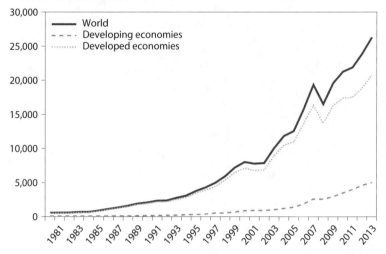

Source: Data from UNCTADstat Database, Foreign Direct Investment Flows and Stock,
http://unctadstat.unctad.org/wds/ReportFolders/reportfolders.aspx.

Fear in advanced countries stems from the new competition in product markets and investment. In 2008 Tata Motors of India acquired Jaguar
Land Rover for $2.3 billion—slightly less than what Ford paid for Jaguar
alone in 1990. A bigger surprise than the purchase itself was the fact that
Tata was far more successful than Ford was in reorganizing the company.
In just a few years, sales tripled and 9,000 employees were added, and Tata
plans to hire more.

In 2004 Ambev, a Brazilian brewer, merged with Interbrew of Belgium
to access European markets. Initially, Inbev, the combined company, had
a European head, but within about a year a Brazilian, Carlos Brito, took
over. Belgium's economy minister bemoaned the fact that the company
was "totally Belgian, then it was Belgian-Brazilian, and now it's Brazilian-
Belgian."[2] Brito is known for his cost cutting (gone were the days of a plush
senior management floor and free cases of beer for employees). His efforts
helped Anheuser-Busch Inbev more than double its stock price after the
2008 merger with Anheuser-Busch despite a stagnant US beer market.

Acquisitions of advanced-country multinationals by emerging-market
firms are becoming common. Saudi Basic Industries Corporation acquired

---

2. Tim Bowler, "The Brazilian Recipe for Brewing Success," BBC, July 14, 2008.

Figure 5.6 Correlation between density of ultra-high-net-worth population and stage of development, 2013

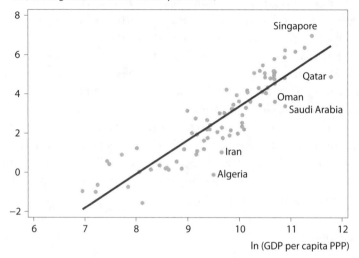

ln (ultra-high-net-worth individuals per million)

Source: Knight Frank (2014).

GE Plastics; Russian company Severstal bought Rouge Steel (US) and Lucchini (Italy). According to the United Nations Conference on Trade and Development (UNCTAD), outward foreign direct investment (FDI) from emerging markets increased nearly sixfold between 2000 and 2014, about twice the increase from developed countries, to account for 20 percent of the total stock of FDI (figure 5.5 located on page 96).

Is Extreme Wealth Necessary?

Entrepreneurs and mega firms are the source of industrialization. Extreme wealth is, therefore, part of development, especially at the beginning of the process, as countries achieve middle-income status. But is extreme wealth necessary? Is it possible to build big productive firms without a few individuals taking such an enormous (and seemingly unfair) share of the pie?

It is very hard to find examples of expanding country income without the emergence of extreme wealth. Across countries the stage of development and the presence of extreme wealth are very highly correlated (see also chapter 4).

Figure 5.6 shows ultra-high-net-worth density and GDP per capita in purchasing power parity (PPP). Data on ultra-high-net-worth people (defined as people worth $30 million or more) include more countries than billionaire data, because many small countries have no billionaires. The high-income countries that fall farthest below the fitted line (where countries are rich but there are few billionaires) are the oil-rich countries in the Gulf. Although these countries are rich, they have failed to industrialize outside of oil, and new businesses in other sectors are not growing or developing significant ties with the rest of the world. Most billionaires are royals, who do not show up in the data. Aside from families with access to oil wealth, there are very few superrich. The region lacks the company founders and executives who create new products and processes.

Singapore is at the opposite extreme of the oil-rich countries. Until recently it was poor, but thanks to its openness to trade and investment, it now has more millionaires per capita than any other economy in the world. With a population of just 5 million, it hosts 16 billionaires. Most are self-made, and many own innovative businesses. Sam Goi, the "popiah king" (described in chapter 3), is one of them.

Takeaways

As startups grow into mega firms and wealth expands, firms pull resources out of agriculture and put them in industry. These firms create better jobs for a country's population and more opportunities for advancement. This process is different in advanced countries, where resources are already largely in industry and services. The expansion of extreme wealth in advanced countries is associated with a shift of labor out of industry into services.

6

Globalization and Extreme Wealth

Martua Sitorus of Indonesia made his fortune in agribusiness. The company he cofounded, Wilmar International, is the world's largest producer of palm oil. It has 450 manufacturing plants in 15 countries and a multinational workforce of about 90,000 people. Eighty percent of the company's revenues come from countries outside Southeast Asia. Eggon João da Silva of Brazil made his fortune in manufacturing. He cofounded WEG, the largest producer of electric motors in Latin America, in 1961. WEG employs more than 27,000 people worldwide and manufactures 11.5 million motors a year. Half of its revenues come from outside Brazil. Global markets are also important for He Xiangjian of China. His fortune stems from the appliance producer Midea, which earns about half of its revenues from exports.

This chapter presents anecdotal evidence that expanding through trade has allowed emerging-market companies to grow faster and larger, enriching their owners. It goes on to examine the relationship between a company's reliance on international markets and the owner's wealth—and also between the amount of extreme wealth in a country and its external linkages. Companies that have a greater share of revenue from outside the home country have richer owners, and countries more open to trade have more billionaires. The chapter discusses the importance of foreign markets, imported inputs, and global supply chains in the creation of extreme wealth in emerging markets. As tariffs and trade costs have fallen and technology has improved, it has become easier to create global factories, which produce internationally and serve customers around the world. The promise of large markets and the efficiency gains from global supply chains have become the blueprint for many large emerging-market multinationals.

Extreme Wealth and Extreme Talent

Theory suggests that when countries integrate through trade, goods prices equalize across countries, which in turn affects wages and the returns to capital. For example, if T-shirt prices in the United States and China are equalized when the two countries trade, then the wages of apparel workers should also converge. More broadly, if goods that use unskilled labor intensively in production (such as light manufactures) are imported at a relatively low price, the demand for unskilled workers falls, putting downward pressure on their wages. Looking for evidence of this so-called Stolper-Samuelson effect (named after the economists who discovered it) has been a major endeavor of trade economists.[1] Empirical studies, however, find that trade plays at most a supporting role in exacerbating income inequality in advanced countries, with technological change being a far more important determinant (see, for example, Edwards and Lawrence 2013). Unlike trade, technological advance directly displaces unskilled labor, as routine tasks can be more easily mechanized, reducing the demand for these workers (consider, for example, the elevator operator or the telephone switchboard worker).

The Stolper-Samuelson effect—the bedrock of the trade and wage literature—does not make predictions about extreme wealth. Models that tie globalization to extreme incomes and wealth rely on gradations among workers and the existence of a small number of extraordinarily talented individuals. According to Jonathan Haskel et al. (2012), these people will command extraordinary pay because they are unusually efficient with capital. Technology plays the role of magnifying the importance of talent differences because the best producer can serve more consumers. For example, new massive open online courses (MOOCs) imply that all students of a subject can learn from the most esteemed professors. Some worry that this could lead to a decline in the demand for instructors at all but the top-ranked universities. Globalization magnifies the return to talent because it increases the potential consumer base for tradable goods. In the example of a MOOC, which new technology makes possible, openness to trade means that MOOCs attract students and professors from all over the world, not just a single country. Together technology and global-

---

1. The Stolper-Samuelson theorem states that under certain conditions a rise in the relative price of a good will lead to a rise in the return to the factor that is used most intensively in the production of the good.

ization boost the wages of a small group of highly talented individuals. The key distinction among models that allow for different worker types is that the standard forces of trade that determine the relative wages of skilled workers are muted compared with the effect on a small group of exceptionally talented individuals.

Examples of the Role of Globalization in Wealth Creation

Dilip Shanghvi borrowed 10,000 rupees (about $1,000 in the 1980s) from his father to start a drug company, Sun Pharmaceutical Industries. Shanghvi chose to focus on medications for chronic diseases because the market was very thin in India, with few suppliers, especially of products designed to treat mental illnesses; other companies were focusing on medications to treat acute illnesses. In addition, chronic illnesses meant that demand would be strong and relatively constant.

Sales of Sun Pharma's first product (lithium, used to treat bipolar disorder) began in 1987; exports followed soon after in 1989 but remained limited in the 1990s. One problem was that exporting alone was not the best way to reach the more lucrative international market, especially the US market, where drug prices were much higher but safety and health regulations were more stringent. So in 1997 Shanghvi bought Detroit-based Caraco Pharma, a distressed generics maker that was approved by the US Food and Drug Administration for manufacturing but had no new drug approvals. The purchase allowed Sun to transfer drug technology to Caraco and get a much larger foothold in the US market. The acquisition is striking since one normally thinks of advanced countries, like the United States, exporting technology to subsidiaries in India to produce at a lower price. Shanghvi's strategy was precisely the reverse, exporting Indian technology and producing in the United States to facilitate adherence with cumbersome US regulations. Since turning Caraco into a highly profitable subsidiary, Sun Pharma has completed 11 more such game-changing deals, including six in the United States, one in Israel, and one in Hungary.[2] Sun Pharma now focuses on complex generics, which means it innovates to improve existing drugs (such as by improving the delivery mechanism). This type of innovation has allowed Sun Pharma's products to take market share from name-brand drugs and other generics and expand their international reach.

---

2. *Forbes India*, "Sun Pharma's Dilip Shanghvi has become the stuff of legend," October 17, 2014.

Figure 6.1   International revenue of Sun Pharmaceutical and the wealth of its founder, 2006–14

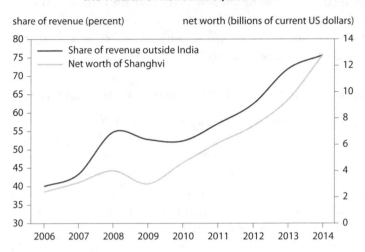

share of revenue (percent)   net worth (billions of current US dollars)

Sources: Data from Forbes, The World's Billionaires; and Revenue by Geography for Sun Pharmaceutical, 2006–2014Q2, Bloomberg (accessed on October 23, 2014).

Shanghvi's wealth soared when his firm expanded globally (figure 6.1), with 75 percent of its 2014 revenue coming from international sales. Today Sun Pharma is the largest drug company in India, employing 16,000 people. In 2014 the company was worth $27 billion, making Shanghvi (worth $12.8 billion) the second-richest man in India.

Luis Matte was a civil engineer involved in the import business in Chile. In 1918 he started a paper company and in 1920 that company merged with German Ebbinghaus to create Compañía Manufacturera de Papeles y Cartones (CMPC). CMPC continued to grow and by 1942 it was supplying Chile with nearly all of its printing and packaging paper. In the 1970s, under the socialist regime of Salvador Allende, the company was the only paper company to escape state control, enabling the opposition newspaper to remain in print.[3] In the 1990s the company moved into Argentina, Peru, and Uruguay. A decade later it expanded to Mexico, Brazil, Ecuador, and Colombia. In this period, the company was at the forefront of technological developments, in terms of both materials produced and reforestation techniques, while investing 70 percent of profits into growth. The share of revenue from outside Chile rose continually and in 2008 increased from less than half to more than 70 percent. The rise in the company's exports

---

3. Funding Universe, "Empresas CMPC S.A. History," www.fundinguniverse.com/company-histories/empresas-cmpc-s-a-history/.

Figure 6.2 International revenue of CMPC and the wealth of its founder and his family, 2007–13

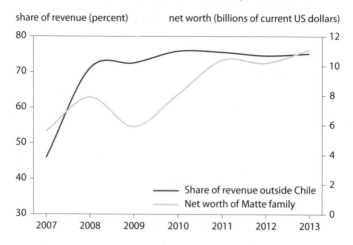

share of revenue (percent)   net worth (billions of current US dollars)

——— Share of revenue outside Chile
········· Net worth of Matte family

2007   2008   2009   2010   2011   2012   2013

Sources: Data from Forbes, The World's Billionaires; and Revenue by Geography for CMPC, 2006–2013, Bloomberg (accessed on October 23, 2014).

corresponded with the growth in the wealth of its owner, Eliodoro Matte, and his family, who own 55 percent of the company (figure 6.2).

Production has also become global. Natura Cosmeticos, the innovative Brazilian cosmetics firm of Antonio Luiz Seabra (discussed in chapter 3), which has been labeled a benefit corporation because of its environmentally sustainable business plan, expanded production into Argentina, Colombia, and Mexico beginning in 2010. The share of exports in its revenues doubled between 2010 and 2013. The company earns 19 percent of revenue abroad and has 400,000 of its 1.7 million consultants (like Avon ladies) outside Brazil.

Trade is increasingly important for all growing companies, not just emerging-market ones. The Swedish retailer H&M, for example, earns only about 5 percent of its revenues in Sweden. Its owners, Stefan and Liselott Persson, depend on external markets for their wealth.

Even billionaires in larger countries are going global. Amancio Ortega was the third-richest person in the world in 2014. The Spaniard first appeared on the Forbes World's Billionaires List in 2001, when his company, Inditex, was listed. Since then his wealth has increased by a factor of 10, reaching $64 billion in 2014. His success is typically attributed to the affordable fashionable style associated with his Zara brand and the vertical integration of his company, which extends from design to production to logistics and retail. But it was developments in trade and technology that made this model possible.

Figure 6.3 Inditex's domestic and international stores and the wealth of its founder, 1994–2013

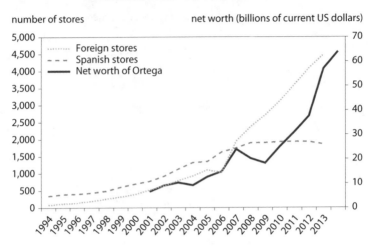

Sources: Inditex annual reports and Forbes, The World's Billionaires.

The combination of a complete shift in trade policy on apparel and improved technology that promoted supply chain development is evident in Zara's rise. Average most-favored nation (MFN) clothing tariffs fell from 18 to 10 percent in advanced countries between 1988 and 2011. Nontariff barriers were also removed. The loosening and the 2004 expiration of the Multifiber Agreement (which had placed strict limits on the quantities of clothing produced in developing countries that could be sold in developed countries) made it increasingly possible to produce at low costs in countries like Morocco and Turkey and sell unlimited quantities in countries like Japan and the United States. Zara's business model relies on maintaining and using information in real time, adjusting production to demand, and shipping goods to more than 6,000 stores worldwide. Technological developments and improved trade facilitation allowed the company to do so.

Figure 6.3 shows Ortega's net wealth and the global and local expansion of his brand. His wealth closely tracks Inditex's global expansion, not its presence in Spain. Had Ortega relied solely on Spanish sales, he would have become very rich. But it was conquering the much larger world market that made him the third-richest person in the world.

While the global market is especially important for emerging markets and small countries, where domestic demand is unlikely to allow the most productive firms to reach their full potential, it is also important for large-country firms, which are increasing their foreign presence to grow. In 1994 Microsoft earned three-quarters of its revenue in the United States; in 2013

Table 6.1   Billionaires connected to major Apple suppliers, 2014

Billionaire	Company	2014 net worth (billions of US dollars)	Citizenship
Terry Gou	Hon Hai Precision Industries (Foxconn)	5.4	Taiwanese
Pan Zhengmin	AAC Technologies	2.6	Chinese
Naruatsu Baba	COLOPL Inc.	2.2	Japanese
Taizo Son	GungHo Online Entertainment	2.1	Japanese
Koo Bon-Moo and Koo Bon-Neung	LG Group	1.5 1.1	Korean

Note: Major suppliers include companies in which 30 to 60 percent of revenue came from sales to Apple in the first three quarters of 2014.

Source: Apple Supply Chain Analysis, percent of revenue, 2014Q1–Q3, Bloomberg (accessed on October 23, 2014).

the United States accounted for just half of the company's earnings, indicating that global sales grew much more rapidly than domestic sales. In 1994 less than 1 percent of Walmart stores were outside the United States; by 2014 the figure had risen to 60 percent.

Trickle-Down Wealth

Because of the integration of production, extreme wealth often spreads from its source in advanced countries to other (mostly emerging) markets along the supply chain. Consider the case of Apple. Forty percent of the company's stores were outside the United States in 2013, but revenue is not the only side of Apple's balance sheet that is globalized. Apple's supply chain extends around the world. The most competitive of Apple's suppliers have become large multinational companies, and their founders have become extremely wealthy. In 2014 Taiwan-based firms controlled about 60 percent of the value associated with the relationship between Apple and its suppliers, with US suppliers representing only 15 percent. Apple also sources from suppliers in Europe, South Africa, and Peru (map 6.1).

Apple is connected to 60 billionaires worldwide. For most of them, revenue from sales to Apple represents less than 5 percent of their revenue in 2014. For six billionaires (connected to five companies), at least 30 percent of revenue comes from sales to Apple. The two richest of these billionaires are from emerging-market companies (table 6.1).[4]

---

4. Zhou Qunfei, of Lens Technology, in China, was added to the list in 2015.

Map 6.1 Apple suppliers by home country, 2014

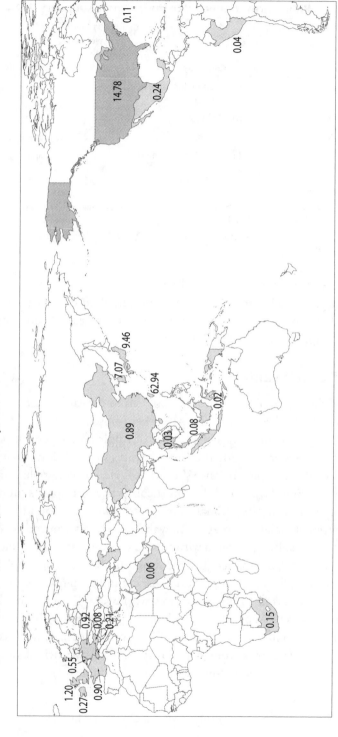

Note: Map shows percent of total supplier relationship value in all countries that host Apple suppliers, based on Bloomberg's assessment of the dollar amount involved in the relationship between suppliers headquartered in each country and Apple. Europe-based suppliers as a whole represent 3.86 percent of total supplier value.

Source: Apple Supply Chain Analysis, relationship value, 2014Q1–Q3, Bloomberg (accessed October 23, 2014).

Table 6.2 Globalization of largest nonfinancial companies as measured by share of international revenue, by region, 2013

Region	Average share of revenue from outside of home country (percent)	Number of companies
Emerging markets		
South Asia	73.1	6
Latin America	72.4	5
Europe	58.2	9
East Asia	16.5	9
China	13.7	6
Total	50.7	29
Total excluding China	60.4	23
Advanced countries		
Europe	79.5	13
Asia	59.1	2
Anglo[a]	42.4	12
Total	61.5	27

a. Anglo countries are the United States, Canada, Australia, and New Zealand.

Note: Sub-Saharan Africa, which had just one company, is not included.

Source: Revenue by Geography 2013, Bloomberg (accessed on October 23, 2014).

Company Exports, Country Trade, and Wealth

How important are global markets for the largest multinational companies that generate extreme wealth? Bloomberg provides financial data on publicly traded companies around the world, and combining these data with the 2014 Forbes World's Billionaires List allows identification of the companies associated with the 50 richest (nonfinancial) billionaires in emerging markets and the companies associated with the 50 richest (nonfinancial) billionaires in advanced countries. Geographically segmented revenue data are available for companies in 33 emerging markets and 27 advanced countries for 2004–14 (though not all companies had data every year), which allows the identification of the share of revenues from international sales.[5] As most company data are in local currencies, international revenue as a share of total revenue was used to make data comparable across countries.

On average large companies are very international, with more than half their revenue coming from exports (table 6.2). Companies in advanced

---

5. Appendix table 6A.1 lists the companies in the sample.

Figure 6.4   Correlation between exports as share of company's revenue and billionaire owner's real net worth, 2004–14

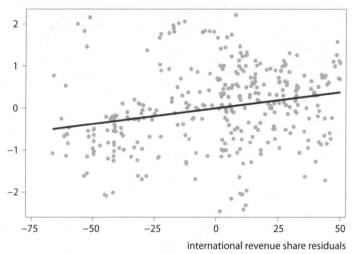

real net worth residual

international revenue share residuals

Note: The vertical axis shows net worth that is not explained by country size (residuals from a regression of individual net worth on home country GDP) and the horizontal axis shows the international revenue share of the company that is not explained by country size (residuals from a regression of international share on home country GDP). Years vary by company.

Sources: Revenue by Geography 2013, Bloomberg (accessed October 23, 2014); and Forbes, The World's Billionaires.

countries tend to derive a larger share of their revenues from exports (62 percent) than companies in emerging markets (51 percent). Regionally, the most globalized firms are in Latin America, South Asia, and developed Europe; companies in developing East Asia are the least global.

It is not surprising that a large share of European firms' revenue is foreign, given the relatively small domestic markets in European countries and the close integration of countries within Europe (trading with another European country counts as global). In contrast, Chinese firms serve a large domestic market. Unlike Google and Facebook, both of which earn more than half of their total revenue outside the United States, Chinese technology companies such as Tencent, Baidu, and Alibaba rely almost exclusively on domestic consumers, with average shares of foreign revenue in 2013 of 7.3, 0.2, and 12.1 percent, respectively. Other East Asian countries look much more like Korea and Japan, where mega firms earn about 60 percent of revenue abroad.

By definition global companies have a larger market than domestic ones, allowing owners to expand wealth. Figure 6.4 shows the relationship

Figure 6.5 Correlation between changes in billionaire wealth and changes in international trade in the billionaire's country, 1996–2014

annual change in net worth of billionaires (percent)

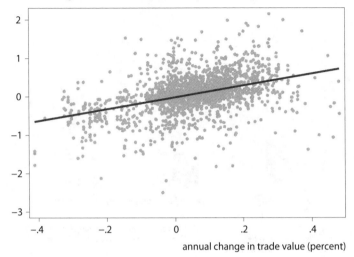

annual change in trade value (percent)

Sources: Data from World Bank, *World Development Indicators*; and Forbes, The World's Billionaires.

between the combined net worth of individuals associated with a company and the international sales share of the company, controlling for country size. It shows that international sales are positively correlated with net worth. Controlling for country size, individuals who expand their companies abroad tend to be richer than those who focus on the domestic market, with a 1 percentage point increase in the international share associated with about a 0.8 percent increase in wealth. This effect is greater than the effect of domestic income (a 1 percent increase in GDP corresponds to only a 0.3 percent increase in wealth).

Given the importance of international markets and imported inputs, countries in which trade is growing faster are likely to be the ones where fortunes are soaring. Even companies that serve domestic markets benefit from trade, because it allows them to use imported inputs.

Figure 6.5 plots the annual growth in billionaire wealth against the annual growth in trade in the billionaire's country. The fitted line shows the strong positive correlation between the two variables.

Trade is also correlated with income growth; trade and net worth could therefore be strongly correlated because both trade and net worth increase when income grows. To explore the role of trade as opposed to broader

Figure 6.6   Relationship between trade, GDP, and billionaire wealth in advanced countries and emerging economies, 1996–2013

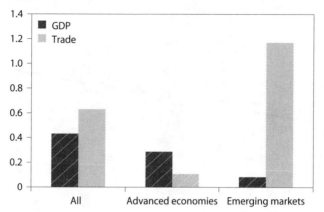

Note: Bars represent coefficients on GDP and trade from a regression of ln(net worth) on ln(income), ln(trade), and country and industry-year fixed effects. Solid bars indicate significance at the 10 percent level.

Source: Author's calculations.

income growth, the correlation between wealth and trade can be evaluated, controlling for standard determinants of wealth. In particular, income, as well as fixed effects for country and industry-year, are included in a regression of net worth on trade.[6] Country fixed effects pick up country characteristics that do not vary with time. For example, the United States may have more billionaires than Brazil because it is larger and is at a higher level of development—or because Forbes is located in the United States and journalists do a better job of tracking wealth there. Industry-year fixed effects pick up changes over time that drive global wealth at the sector level, such as the effect of rising commodity prices on resources.

The net worth data are at the country-industry level. The five industries are resources, traded goods, nontraded goods, new sectors, and finance.

Figure 6.6 presents the results. It shows that wealth is positively and significantly associated with trade in the full sample. Although positive,

---

6. The dependent variable is aggregate annual country-industry net worth from 1996 to 2013, the most recent year for which *World Development Indicators* data are available. The independent variables are income, country fixed effects, industry fixed effects, and year fixed effects. Trade, income, and net worth are in real terms and in logs. Errors are clustered at the country level.

the effect is not statistically significant in the North. The correlation between trade and wealth is much stronger in the South.

The results indicate that increased trade is closely related to the increase in wealth in emerging markets. The coefficient is just over 1, meaning that a 1 percent increase in a country's trade is associated with about a 1 percent increase in the net worth of billionaires, after controlling for income growth in the country and country-specific and industry-specific effects. This result is similar to the relationship found using company data. Trade in emerging markets grew on average 7.4 percent a year over the period. Using the estimated coefficient of 1 on the log of trade implies that growth in real trade contributed to an annual increase in billionaire wealth of 7.4 percent. The average annual increase in real wealth in emerging markets was 10.7 percent, suggesting that 70 percent of the increase in the wealth of billionaires was related to trade growth.

The statistically insignificant effects of both trade and income in the advanced countries are at first perplexing. But separating the regressions by sector explains why trade and GDP are less important in the North than in the South. Wealth associated with finance exhibits a strong negative correlation with trade in the North. Excluding finance, the coefficient on trade (0.60) is positive and significant. This result suggests that the rise of extreme wealth in the North is more closely related to developments in the domestic financial sector than to globalization, an issue addressed in chapter 10.

Takeaways

Trade explains much of the rise of extreme wealth in emerging markets. Although the share of foreign revenues is higher in advanced-country mega firms, the rate of increase of international revenues is faster among emerging-market firms, as they are rapidly expanding their foreign presence, and thus trade is a bigger contributor to recent wealth creation in emerging markets. Increases in the home country's trade can explain about 70 percent of the rise in extreme wealth in the South. The extraordinary rise in the wealth of emerging-market billionaires is to a large extent the result of having a wider selection of resources to use in production and a large market to sell to.

Appendix 6A

Table 6A.1   List of companies in emerging-market and advanced economies with the richest billionaire owners, by nonfinancial sector, 2014

Type of sector	Emerging markets		Advanced countries	
	Company	Country	Company	Country
Resource-related	Antofagasta PLC	Chile	Continental Resources	United States
	Aditya Birla Group	India		
	ArcelorMittal	India		
	Reliance	India		
	Grupo México	Mexico		
	Peñoles	Mexico		
	Gazprom	Russia		
	Lukoil	Russia		
	Metalloinvest	Russia		
	NLMK	Russia		
	Norilsk Nickel	Russia		
	Novatek	Russia		
	Severstal	Russia		
New technologies	Alibaba Group	China	Serono	Switzerland
	Baidu	China	Synthes USA	Switzerland
	Tencent	China	Dassault Group	France
	Hanergy Solar	China	Alliance Boots	Switzerland
	HCL	India	SoftBank	Japan
	Sun Pharmaceutical Industries	India	Samsung	Korea
	Wipro Limited	India	Amazon	United States
			Apple	United States
			Dell	United States
			Facebook	United States
			Google	United States
			Microsoft	United States
			Oracle	United States

(table continues)

Table 6A.1 List of companies in emerging-market and advanced economies with the richest billionaire owners, by nonfinancial sector, 2014 *(continued)*

	Emerging markets		Advanced countries	
Type of sector	Company	Country	Company	Country
Nontraded	Grupo Globo	Brazil	Kering	France
	Chow Tai Fook Enterprises	Hong Kong	Dish Network	United States
	Grupo Elektra	Mexico	News Limited	United States
	Telmex	Mexico	Walmart	United States
	Magnit	Russia		
	Sistema	Russia		
Traded	Ambev	Brazil	BMW	Germany
	Great Wall Motors	China	L'Oréal	France
	Dangote Group	Nigeria	Hinduja Group	United Kingdom
	Uralkali	Russia	Armani	Italy
	Want Want China	Taiwan	Prada	Italy
	Charoen Pokphand (CP) Group	Thailand	Luxottica	Italy
	ThaiBev	Thailand	Fast Retailing (Uniqlo)	Japan
			Heineken International	Netherlands
			Nike	United States

Note: These companies are associated with the 50 richest individuals in nonfinancial sectors in both emerging markets and advanced economies in 2014 and represent the companies for which geographically segmented company revenue data are available.

Source: Revenue by Geography 2004–14, Bloomberg (accessed on October 23, 2014).

III

DEMOGRAPHIC DIFFERENCES

7

A Few Good Women

Zhou Qunfei grew up poor in Hunan Province, where she worked on her family's farm to help support her family. Later, while working at a factory in Guangdong Province, she took business and computer courses at Shenzhen University. She started a company with money she saved working for a watch producer. In 2015 she was the world's richest self-made woman, with a fortune of $5.3 billion, according to Forbes. Her wealth comes from her company, Lens Technology, which makes touchscreens. It employs 60,000 people and has a market capitalization of nearly $12 billion.

Lei Jufang was born in Gansu Province, one of the poorest areas of northwest China. After studying physics at Jiao Tong University, she created a new method for vacuum packaging food and drugs, which won her acclaim as an assistant professor. On a trip to Tibet she became fascinated by herbal medicines. In 1995 she founded a drug company, Cheezheng Tibetan Medicine, harnessing her skill in physics and engineering to exploit the untapped market for Tibetan medicine. Her company has a research institute and three factories that produce herbal healing products for consumers in China, Malaysia, Singapore, and North and South America. She has amassed a fortune of $1.5 billion.

In most countries, women get rich by inheriting money. China is different: The majority of its women billionaires are self-made. Zhou Qunfei and Lei Jufang are unusual because they established their own companies. Most of the eight Chinese female self-made company founders worth more than $1 billion made their money in real estate or in companies founded jointly with husbands or brothers.

Women made up less than 3 percent of all self-made billionaires in emerging markets in 2014. Of the five richest women in these markets—Iris Fontbona, Yang Huiyan, Eva Gonda Rivera, Pansy Ho, and Chan Laiwa—four inherited their fortunes. Two are from Latin America (Chile and Mexico), two from Mainland China, and one from Hong Kong. The fifth-richest, Chan Laiwa, is the founder of the Chinese real estate company Fu Wah International Group.

Self-made female billionaires are equally scarce in advanced countries, where women also account for less than 3 percent of the total. All five of the richest women from advanced countries—Christy Walton, Liliane Bettencourt, Alice Walton, Jacqueline Mars, and Gina Rinehart—inherited their fortunes, although Rinehart, the Australian mining magnate, heads her company and expanded her fortune dramatically.

The Amazing Women of China and the United States

Of the 38 female self-made billionaires in the world in 2014, 16 are from the United States (3.2 percent of all self-made billionaires there) and 8 are from China (5.2 percent of all self-made billionaires there). The United Kingdom is home to three, and Hong Kong has two. Angola, Brazil, Italy, Kazakhstan, South Korea, Macau, Nigeria, and Russia each have one. In 2001 only three women, all from advanced economies, were self-made billionaires.

These women are not as rich as their male counterparts. In emerging markets their average net worth is $1.1 billion less than that of self-made men; in advanced countries the difference is even larger ($1.7 billion).

The share of female billionaires in the North is about twice the share in the South, and the size of both groups roughly doubled in 2001–14 (table 7.1). The share of female self-made billionaires in emerging markets is about the same as in advanced countries. In both regions the share of inherited wealth among women increased between 2001 and 2014. Women remain grossly underrepresented in all categories of billionaires.

Sectors of Self-Made Women

Half of all self-made billionaire women in emerging markets made their money in the financial sector. This figure is significantly larger than the figure for men (35 percent) (table 7.2). In contrast, in the North women are underrepresented in the financial sector. The difference may be in part because finance in the South is primarily real estate, while in the North it is investment banking and hedge funds. In both the traded and nontraded

Table 7.1 Distribution of male and female billionaires and their wealth in advanced countries and emerging markets, 2001 and 2014 (percent of total)

Type of wealth/gender	2001		2014	
	Share of all billionaires	Share of all billionaire wealth	Share of all billionaires	Share of all billionaire wealth
Advanced countries				
Inherited				
Men	34.7	33.4	26.7	29.1
Women	7.1	10.7	11.0	12.4
Self-made				
Men	57.5	55.4	60.1	57.3
Women	0.7	0.5	2.2	1.2
Emerging markets				
Inherited				
Men	41.8	41.8	16	17.5
Women	4.1	2.9	5.1	4.2
Self-made				
Men	54.1	55.3	76.6	76.8
Women	0	0	2.3	1.5

Source: Author's classification based on data from Forbes, The World's Billionaires.

sectors, women tend to be more prevalent in areas traditionally associated with them, such as fashion and health care, and tend to be less prevalent in areas requiring heavy startup investments, such as machinery. In both the North and the South, women underperform in the resource sector. Resource wealth is typically connected to the government (which grants rights and permits), suggesting that women may be excluded from certain networks. The list of company founders includes only 19 women who are not in finance or politically connected (12 in the United States, 4 in China, and 3 in Europe) (table 7.3). Even within this elite group, the vast majority started their companies with their husbands or brothers. Only six founded their companies alone.

Table 7.2 Source of wealth of male and female self-made billionaires in advanced countries and emerging markets, 2014 (percent of total)

Sector	Men	Women
Advanced countries		
Resource-related	6.8	0
New	17.6	23.8
Nontraded	23.1	38.1
Traded	15.8	28.6
Financial	34.6	9.5
Other	2.1	0
Emerging markets		
Resource-related	16.0	6.3
New	11.8	12.5
Nontraded	15.6	18.8
Traded	20.5	12.5
Financial	35.2	50.0
Other	0.9	0

Source: Author's classification based on data from Forbes, The World's Billionaires.

Why Are There So Few Self-Made Billionaire Women?

One reason there are so few women billionaires may be that a woman needs to persevere more to break into a new business because of discrimination or exclusion at all levels of product development. The story of American billionaire Sara Blakely, the founder of Spanx, which makes women's undergarments, highlights the constraints women face. Blakely cut off the legs of her pantyhose to achieve a smoother look under pants while still being able to wear open-toed shoes. Other women had probably done this before, but she recognized that the idea was marketable and acted on it. She spent two years developing the product, which she brought to market while working a day job. She stayed engaged with all aspects of the business, even moving the placement of the product in department stores to ensure sales. Her big break came when another female billionaire, Oprah Winfrey, identified Spanx as a favorite product. Blakely financed development largely from retained earnings. To this day she owns 100 percent of the company.

Table 7.3 Companies founded or cofounded by women who became billionaires, by region, 2014

Country/name	Net worth (billions of dollars)	Industry	Company	Founding date	Cofounded
China					
Chu Lam Yiu (Hong Kong)	1.8	Flavorings	Huabao International Holdings	1990	Yes
He Qiaonu	1.5	Landscape design	Beijing Orient Landscape	1992	No
Lei Jufang	1.4	Pharmaceuticals	Tibet Cheezheng Tibetan Medicine	1993	No
Cheung Yan	1.1	Paper	Nine Dragons Paper	1995	Yes
Europe					
Rafaela Aponte (Switzerland)	3.2	Shipping	MSC	1970	Yes
Giuliana Benetton (Italy)	2.9	Apparel	Benetton Group	1965	Yes
Denise Coates (United Kingdom)	1.6	Gaming	Bet365	2000	No

(table continues)

121

Table 7.3 Companies founded or cofounded by women who became billionaires, by region, 2014 (*continued*)

Country/name	Net worth (billions of dollars)	Industry	Company	Founding date	Cofounded
United States					
Gayle Cook	5.8	Medical technology	Cook Group	1963	Yes
Diane Hendricks	4.6	Roofing	ABC Supply	1982	Yes
Doris Fisher	3.3	Apparel	The Gap	1969	Yes
Judy Faulkner	3.1	Healthcare software	Epic Systems	1979	No
Jin Sook Chang	2.9	Apparel	Forever 21	1984	Yes
Oprah Winfrey	2.9	Media	Harpo Productions	1986	No
Johnelle Hunt	2.1	Trucking	J.B. Hunt Transport Services	1961	Yes
Marian Ilitch	1.8	Restaurant	Little Caesars Pizza	1959	Yes
Judy Love	1.8	Truck stops	Love's Travel Stops & Country Stores	1964	Yes
Peggy Cherng	1.4	Restaurant	Panda Express	1973	Yes
Sara Blakely	1.0	Apparel	Spanx	2000	No
Tory Burch	1.0	Apparel	Tory Burch LLC	2004	Yes

Note: List excludes women who made their fortune in finance or through political connections.

Source: Author's classification based on data from Forbes, The World's Billionaires.

Three features of this story stand out: innovation and perseverance, a lucky break with an important business connection that yields access to potential customers, and very limited financing. These features are common to the stories of many women billionaires.

Kiran Mazumdar-Shaw, India's only self-made female billionaire, also experienced a lucky break. After struggling to find a position as a brew-master in the traditionally male-dominated brewing industry in India, she met an Irish entrepreneur looking to bring biotech to India, who persuaded her to switch from beer to enzyme production. Her first outside investment was granted at a social event, after banks refused to loan money.

The more business connections a person has, the more likely he or she is to get that lucky break. Women tend to have fewer links with industrial counterparts than men. Across countries they are less prevalent in the C-suite and corporate boards and outnumbered in industrial organizations, and only a small number hold top government positions, especially in business-related areas (Kotschwar and Moran 2015).

Paul Gompers et al. (2014) study female venture capitalists (VCs) to highlight the importance of networks. They show that male VCs benefit from successful colleagues but female VCs do not if their colleagues are all male (as is often the case). Women significantly underperform male colleagues with similar characteristics, but the performance gap is due to the quality of a man's male colleagues. The authors' interviews indicate that women do not participate in informal meetings and social activities to the same extent as men. As one woman commented, "There are many events for VCs...that don't include women. Fly fishing, car racing, golf, etc.—no women." Another VC noted that she was "often inadvertently excluded from a variety of social gatherings, including guys' weekends." This networking effect, which is very important in the financial sector, may help explain why so few women made their fortunes in finance (outside of real estate) and why women entrepreneurs have a harder time accessing finance.

Difficulty obtaining financing means that companies must grow first, before or without ever receiving the large financial backing typically needed to turn a company into a global powerhouse. Financing is also important for growth, especially in industries where startup costs are high. Research shows that external financing is less available to women even in the United States. According to the Diana Project, which studies women's entrepreneurship, "while the rate of women's participation in new venture creation around the world was at an all-time high during the 1990s, their ability to grow their companies by accessing equity capital was extremely limited. Nearly 20 percent of the IPOs brought to market from 1995–1998 were women-owned or managed firms, providing evidence of women's ability to lead high-growth, high-value firms, yet only 2 percent of these were venture funded" (Brush et al. 2004, 2). A wealth of studies from the World Bank, summarized in its *Gender at Work* report (2014), shows that women entrepreneurs in developing countries tend to be especially underserved by the financial sector.

The problem with obtaining finance for a new enterprise is in part associated with the small number of female investors. Only 6 percent of VCs in the United States are women and nearly 80 percent of firms have never had a female investor (Gompers et al. 2014).

Why Is China Different?

China's relative success in female entrepreneurship is credited to a number of factors. One is culture: In China, unlike many other developing countries, women are expected to work outside the home. Like in the United States, women make up nearly half of the labor force; the ratio of women's participation to men's participation is 82 percent in both countries, according to the World Bank (2012). There are also more opportunities for innovative women like Lei Jufang because of growth and modernization. In addition, most private firms in China grow through retained earnings (Lardy 2014), so competition from well-financed firms is less intense.

Importance of Female Entrepreneurs for Resource Allocation

The problem of the dearth of female entrepreneurs goes beyond equity: The small number of female mega firm founders implies that some great ideas are not being exploited. Discrimination is not just a problem for the people it directly affects; it hurts the economy as a whole. There is no reason to think that half of the population has less than 3 percent of the best business ideas. The fact that women have a harder time joining business networks and finding financing makes it harder for them to grow their companies. Worse still, it discourages other women from even trying to start a business. If women were part of business networks and had equal access to finance, there would very likely be more new businesses, more competition, and a better allocation of capital. Indeed, the two countries with the most women on the list, the United States and China, are arguably the best-performing countries in their income brackets. Raising hurdles for female entrepreneurs lowers the bar for potential firm growth, reducing job opportunities.

Women Helping Women

An encouraging sign for future growth is that women who strike it rich often help other women. US billionaire women Tory Burch and Sara Blakely owe their success to the most famous American female billionaire, Oprah Winfrey. Her endorsement of their products marked the turning points in growth for their companies, highlighting the importance of business networks. Winfrey is helping women in many other ways as well, and not just in the United States. Her foundation focuses on girls in South Africa.

Burch and Blakely are following her lead. Both the Tory Burch Foundation and Leg Up (Blakely's foundation) support women entrepreneurs through loans and training. Sheryl Sandberg, the second-most famous American female billionaire, is also interested in women's issues. Her bestseller, *Lean In*, is about what women can do for themselves to improve chances of career promotion and business success and also the gains from company and country policies that encourage leadership in women.

Outside the United States, many women who have made large fortunes contribute to causes that support women and children. Folorunsho Alakija, Nigeria's richest woman, created the Rose of Sharon Foundation, which provides widows and orphans with business grants and scholarships. Lei Jufang has set up schools in Tibet that train students, mostly from poor backgrounds, to be doctors. Giuliana Benetton and her siblings have created a charity to help children in war-torn areas. J. K. Rowling, the author of the Harry Potter series, contributed so much of her fortune to charities to help women and children that she dropped off the Forbes World's Billionaires List in 2012.

Why Do Women Inherit Less Than Men?

Women represent a relatively small share of inherited wealth—less than a third of the spots for heirs in both the North and the South. Their underrepresentation may reflect a preference for passing wealth on to male relatives.

Some family fortunes have been divided equally. Patricia and Roberto Angelini Rossi cochair the Angelini Group. The three billionaire children of Samsung chair Lee Kun-Hee all have leadership roles in the company (though only his son has been groomed to take his position). Catherine Lozick's father left her, not her brother, the majority stake in his water valve company (Swagelok). Globally, however, less than 30 percent of inherited billionaires are female, suggesting that either parents leave larger shares of their fortunes to their sons or men are more likely to grow or maintain a large inheritance (the significantly larger number of self-made male billionaires is consistent with the notion that men are more successful than women at expanding fortunes).

But there is evidence that daughters are often shortshrifted when it comes to inheritance. In countries with at least five inherited fortunes, Egypt, Singapore, and Taiwan report none accruing to women, and Canada, the United Kingdom, and Italy record female inherited wealth at 15 percent or less of total inherited wealth. Studies of family businesses in countries as different as Denmark and Thailand show strong evidence of bias toward passing on ownership to men over women (Bennedsen, Pérez-González, and Wolfenzon 2007; Bertrand et al. 2008).

Takeaways

Large-scale entrepreneurship among women is extremely rare. The United States and China have performed the best, but even in these countries there are more than nine self-made male billionaires for every female one.

Weaker business networks and limited access to financing help explain the small share of women leading large businesses. Women have tended to grow companies in areas with large shares of female consumers, such as fashion, food, health care, and services, where networks for female entrepreneurs are stronger and significant financing is not a requirement to start up. In contrast, there are no female company founders in machinery, electronics, or hedge funds.

The absence of women is not just bad from an equitable distribution perspective. It has implications for resource allocation—the theme of this book. A great deal of talent appears to be going to waste. The higher bars that women have to jump over to grow businesses mean that some great ideas are not being transformed into mega firms and economic growth.

8

Young Entrepreneurs, Younger Firms

New technologies have created a new class of wealth, most of it controlled by young men (and a few women). Thirty-two-year-old Leo Chen of China is the youngest self-made billionaire in the developing world. Bobby Murphy and Evan Spiegel, the creators of Snapchat, became billionaires at 24. Facebook cofounders Mark Zuckerberg and Dustin Moskovitz became billionaires well before 30. Forty-five percent of billionaires under 40 made their fortunes in new technology (82 percent if inherited wealth is excluded).

Except in new technologies, where the superrich from all countries tend to be young, emerging-market billionaires are significantly younger than their advanced-country counterparts, and their firms are newer. More than half of emerging-market billionaires are under 60, compared with less than one-third of advanced-country billionaires.

The sources of their wealth are also young. The average firm of a billionaire from the South was created in 1986, compared with 1967 for his counterpart in the North. Emerging-market billionaires are in the prime of their lives, running relatively new businesses.

Studies of the psychology of extreme wealth find that its creators are often people who are able to spot revolutionary change and act on it. Times of transformation are times when fortunes can be made or lost. Chrystia Freeland writes about this mentality in *Plutocrats: The Rise of the New Global Super-Rich and the Fall of Everyone Else*. Billionaires born in emerging markets, such as George Soros, Aditya Mittal, and Yuri Milner, show a unique ability to spot transformation and make immediate and large investments. As

Freeland puts it, "Responding to revolution is how you become a Pluto-crat" (2012, 162). These people are willing to take huge risks, risks extraor-dinary enough to make billions but risks that sometimes end very badly. (The riches of Lai Changxing and Mikhail Khodorkovsky landed both men in jail.) This leads to high volatility at the top in some countries and, as more than one commentator on the rich has remarked, to extreme para-noia among the rich who survive.

The opportunities created by seismic economic shifts are part of the reason why industrialization and modernization tend to coincide with the emergence of a new class of mega-rich. Structural transformation creates change and opportunity that enables fortunes to be built quickly. To the extent that wealth creation is a natural phenomenon that accompanies change, the billionaires of the developing world may look much more like the young billionaires of advanced countries who mastered new technolo-gies than older billionaires who got rich producing traditional goods. Like the structural transformation in emerging markets, new technologies have created extraordinary opportunities for building companies for those rare individuals who can see the direction of change and have the talent to act on it.

The divergence between North and South in the age of firms associ-ated with large fortunes is relatively new. In 2001 the age of the median firm was similar: 45 in the North and 42 in the South. By 2014 billionaires' firms had aged in the North, with an average age of 47. In contrast, the median firm in the South was just 28 years old, similar to the age of the median new sector firm in the North (31).

This chapter uses founding dates of companies associated with billion-aire wealth to assess the decay of old fortunes and the growth of new fortunes among the superrich. It documents the extent of creative destruction, the process by which more productive firms replace less productive firms.

Emerging-Market Billionaires Are Young

Emerging-market billionaires, particularly self-made, are younger than their advanced-country counterparts (figure 8.1).

In emerging markets, billionaires under 50 outnumber billionaires over 70. The distribution of self-made billionaires is skewed toward young-er billionaires, whereas inherited wealth is more evenly distributed around the mean. In contrast, more than one-third of high-income-country bil-lionaires are 70 years or older, with just 12 percent under 50. In advanced countries the distributions of self-made and inherited billionaires by age are nearly identical.

Figure 8.1   Distribution of billionaires in advanced countries and emerging economies, by age and source of wealth, 2014

a. Advanced countries

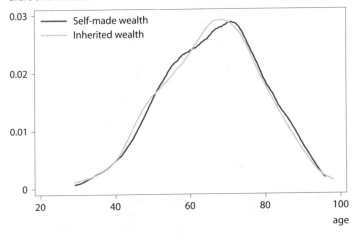

b. Emerging economies

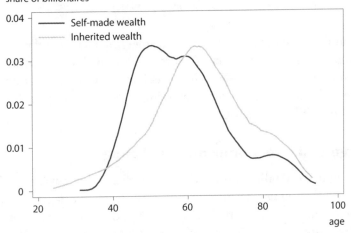

Note: This graph shows the distribution of billionaires at each age, using a smoothed histogram to connect the observations.

Source: Data from Forbes, The World's Billionaires.

Emerging-market billionaires are responding to new opportunities in their economies. They therefore tend to be younger than entrepreneurs from high-income countries. Advanced-country billionaires in new sectors are also responding to rapid technological change and therefore may be

Figure 8.2   Distribution of self-made billionaires in advanced countries and emerging economies, by age and industry, 2014

share of billionaires

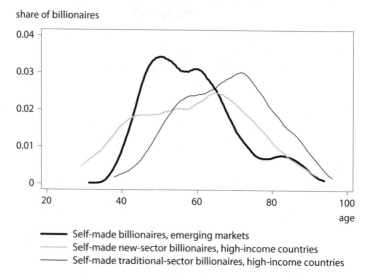

Self-made billionaires, emerging markets
Self-made new-sector billionaires, high-income countries
Self-made traditional-sector billionaires, high-income countries

Note: This graph shows the distribution of billionaires at each age, using a smoothed histogram to connect the observations.

Source: Author's research using data from Forbes, The World's Billionaires.

more similar to self-made billionaires in emerging markets than self-made billionaires in more traditional sectors (both traded and nontraded sectors). Indeed, new-technology billionaires have a wider distribution across ages and they overlap more with emerging-market billionaires than other high-income billionaires (figure 8.2).

Emerging-Market Companies Are Young

Emerging-market billionaires are younger than their advanced-country counterparts, even new-technology billionaires. However, age only approximates the time it takes to build a fortune and does not offer information about inherited wealth. This section therefore looks at the age of fortunes by company founding date.

Of the five oldest companies associated with individuals on the Forbes billionaires list in 2014, three fortunes stem from European nobility. The oldest is that of the von Thurn und Taxis family, who operated the German postal system beginning in 1615.[1] The Canada-based Hudson's

---

1. The other two companies associated with European nobility are Britain's Grosvenor

Bay Company, which began as a fur trading group, is more than 300 years old. China's largest soy sauce producer, the Foshan Haitian Flavouring Company, was founded in the 1700s. Very few fortunes last this long; only 7 percent of companies associated with wealth in 2014 were founded before 1900, down from 13 percent in 2001.

Companies are becoming younger, particularly in emerging markets. Some of the youngest companies on the 2001 billionaires list in high-income economies—including Yahoo! (founded in 1994), Amazon (1994), and eBay (1995)—are today's technology giants. In 2014 the youngest companies in high-income countries were also technology companies, including Groupon (founded in 2008), WhatsApp (2009), and Zulily (2010). In emerging markets the four youngest companies in 2001 were all Russian oil or gas companies, riding the wave of privatization in the country; all of them were at least eight years old. By 2014 the youngest firms were half that age, with Chinese mobile phone company Xiaomi Tech making its founder, Lei Jun, a billionaire only four years after he founded the company, in 2010.

The founding dates of companies offer more precise information about the life cycle of fortunes than the age of billionaires. An average founding year in 2001 that is similar to the average founding year in 2014 is consistent with the idea that the same fortunes remain intact (though the names of owners may change), because of either bequests or investment. A later founding date is consistent with wealth turnover among the superrich and creative destruction among firms.

The average business associated with billionaires was 50 years old in 2014, younger than in 2001, when the average firm was 55 (table 8.1). The median company was also younger in 2014 (41) than in 2001 (43).[2] This could be because of an abundance of young new companies, with the biggest companies and hence the richest individuals remaining the same over time. But stagnancy at the top is not the case: Even among the top 150 billionaires the companies associated with the biggest fortunes were roughly the same age in 2001 and 2014, indicating that new companies moved into

---

Group (1677), associated with the Duke of Westminster, and Cadogan Estates (1712), associated with the Earls Cadogan.

2. In this section information on the main company associated with each fortune as well as the founding date of each primary company is added to the 2001 and 2014 billionaire lists. Each individual rather than each company is counted as an observation. Billionaires whose wealth came from the same company are therefore individual data points.

Table 8.1 Average founding date of billionaire-related companies in advanced countries and emerging economies, 2001 and 2014

Type of wealth	Founding date		25 percent of companies founded	
	Mean	Median	Before	After
2001				
World	1946	1958	1926	1975
Self-made	1967	1971	1959	1982
Inherited	1918	1926	1899	1948
Advanced countries	1946	1959	1926	1975
Self-made	1968	1972	1960	1982
Inherited	1914	1923	1896	1947
Emerging economies	1948	1956	1926	1971
Self-made	1962	1963	1955	1981
Inherited	1932	1935	1919	1955
2014				
World	1964	1973	1949	1991
Self-made	1979	1985	1970	1994
Inherited	1928	1938	1911	1953
Advanced countries	1956	1967	1941	1984
Self-made	1976	1980	1967	1990
Inherited	1923	1936	1903	1951
Emerging economies	1974	1986	1959	1994
Self-made	1983	1991	1975	1995
Inherited	1940	1945	1925	1959

Source: Author's research based on data from Forbes, The World's Billionaires.

the top 150 richest between 2001 and 2014. If the same companies created the biggest fortunes in both years, the companies would have aged by 13 years over the period.

In advanced countries companies tend to be older than emerging-market firms, and they were older in 2014 (average age of 58) than in 2001 (average age of 55). In contrast, emerging-market companies were 12 years younger in 2014 (average age of 40) than in 2001 (average age of 52). Companies in emerging markets associated with self-made billionaires had a median age of 35 in 2001 and 23 in 2014. In advanced countries, the median age was 29 in 2001 and 35 in 2014.

To understand the difference in distribution of founding dates across

Figure 8.3 Age of companies associated with billionaire wealth in advanced countries and emerging economies, 2001 and 2014

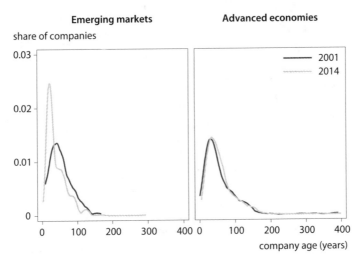

Note: This graph shows the distribution of companies at each age, using a smoothed histogram to connect the observations.

Sources: Author's research using data from Forbes, The World's Billionaires.

years, as well as the influence of outliers, figure 8.3 plots the age of billionaire companies in each year. The vertical axis shows the share of companies of any given age (from the horizontal axis) in that year. Age rather than founding date is plotted to account for the 13-year gap between data. The distribution of company founding dates is indeed right-skewed, with a small share of very old companies pulling the mean company age above the highest concentration of billionaires. The distributions of company age in 2001 and 2014 are very similar in advanced countries, indicating turnover in the companies responsible for billionaire wealth. But a kind of steady-state equilibrium is evident, in which new firms displace older firms at a constant rate, keeping average age fixed. In contrast, in emerging markets there is a shift in the distribution toward younger companies in 2014, with a quarter of all emerging-market companies founded between 1990 and 1995. Excluding China and Russia reduces this concentration of young firms, but the data still show a shift toward younger firms (figure 8.4).

Using founding dates is useful for comparing today's emerging-market entrepreneurs with different types of entrepreneurs in advanced countries. In 2014 the distribution of founding dates of emerging-market compa-

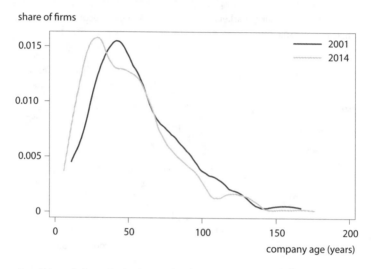

Figure 8.4 Age of companies associated with billionaire wealth in emerging economies, excluding China and Russia, 2001 and 2014

share of firms

Note: This graph shows the distribution of companies at each age, using a smoothed histogram to connect the observations.

Source: Author's research using data from Forbes, The World's Billionaires.

nies in new, traded, and nontraded sectors tracked the distribution of new-sector billionaires in advanced countries, with a peak at about 20 years. In contrast, most billionaire-related companies in traded and nontraded sectors in advanced countries are at least 30 years old (figure 8.5). New-sector firms in advanced countries thus look more like emerging-market firms than other advanced-country firms.

The results are in line with work by Nicolas Véron (2008), who finds that among the top 500 largest companies, emerging-market companies tend to be younger than advanced-country firms. He interprets this finding as reflecting a catch-up growth process. The results above also show that large-scale entrepreneurship is a much more recent phenomenon in emerging markets.

Transition: Get Richer or Get Out

Table 8.2 shows transition matrices for billionaires from the North and the South. Quintile 1 is the bottom 20 percent of billionaires; quintile 5 is the top 20 percent. The matrix shows where the billionaires who were in each quintile in 2001 ended up in 2014.

Figure 8.5   Age of companies associated with billionaire founders in advanced countries and emerging economies, by type of sector, 2014

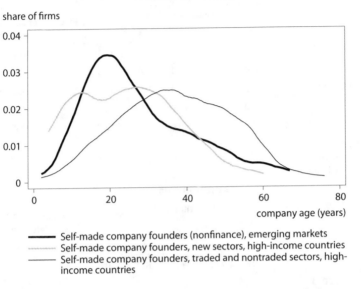

share of firms

company age (years)

——— Self-made company founders (nonfinance), emerging markets
··········· Self-made company founders, new sectors, high-income countries
——— Self-made company founders, traded and nontraded sectors, high-income countries

Note: This graph shows the distribution of companies at each age, using a smoothed histogram to connect the observations.

Source: Author's research using data from Forbes, The World's Billionaires.

The data show a very strong up-or-out phenomenon, especially in the South. No matter where billionaires start in 2001, if they remain on the list, they are much more likely to move up than to stay in the same cohort. Nearly 80 percent of billionaires from emerging markets who started in the bottom quintile in 2001 moved up to the top quintile or exited by 2014, compared with less than 60 percent from advanced countries. Not a single emerging-market billionaire who was on the list and in the bottom quintile in 2001 remained there in 2014 (upper-left entry); all either exited or moved up the distribution.

Thus, changes in the emerging-market billionaires list from 2001 to 2014 reveal tremendous movement. Only 60 percent of the fortunes survived. Of the fortunes in the bottom 20 percent of the distribution in 2001, only half survived. Those that did, however, were twice as likely to move up to the top quintile as they were to remain in the bottom one.

Table 8.2 Movement of billionaires across quintiles in advanced countries and emerging economies, 2001–14

		Emerging economies					
		Quintiles, 2014					Exit (percent of billionaires who left each quintile)
		1	2	3	4	5	
Quintiles, 2001	1	0.0	7.1	3.6	10.7	32.1	46.4
	2	0.0	0.0	14.3	0.0	42.9	42.9
	3	0.0	12.5	0.0	12.5	43.8	31.3
	4	0.0	0.0	11.8	23.5	23.5	41.2
	5	0.0	5.9	0.0	11.8	52.9	29.4
Entry (percent of billionaires who entered each quintile)		24.4	21.6	18	20.7	15.4	

		Advanced countries					
		Quintiles, 2014					Exit (percent of billionaires who left each quintile)
		1	2	3	4	5	
Quintiles, 2001	1	9.0	9.0	13	10.0	5.0	54
	2	9.6	7.2	6.0	18.1	9.6	49.4
	3	4.6	10.2	11.4	12.5	15.9	45.5
	4	5.6	4.4	13.3	20.0	24.4	32.2
	5	1.2	1.2	5.9	9.4	57.7	24.7
Entry (percent of billionaires who entered each quintile)		25.8	21.6	22.6	17.3	12.6	

Source: Author's calculations using data from Forbes, The World's Billionaires.

Creative Destruction: Changes in the Billionaires List between 2001 and 2014

All of the evidence points to more dynamism in the South than in the North. A stability index, which gives a sense of how much turnover there is among top businesses or entrepreneurs, can also be used to determine whether this dynamism is present among the largest firms. Kathy Fogel, Randall Morck, and Bernard Young (2008), for example, examine stability in the top 10 businesses in 1978 and 1998 in a sample of 44 countries. They find that greater turnover among the top businesses in a country is associated with faster economic growth, which they interpret as evidence of creative destruction. Countries perform better when the business sector is more dynamic, with new businesses growing large and replacing aging national champions.

Stability is measured by the share of the top 3, 5, or 10 billionaires on

Table 8.3 Five-year stability index for top 3, top 5, and top 10 billionaires, by country, 2009–14

Top 3 country	Stability index	Top 5 country	Stability index	Top 10 country	Stability index
		Advanced countries			
Canada	0.33	Canada	0.40	Spain	0.30
Japan	0.33	Spain	0.40	Canada	0.40
Norway	0.33	United Kingdom	0.40	Germany	0.50
Australia	0.67	Japan	0.40	France	0.50
Austria	0.67	Australia	0.60	Italy	0.50
Germany	0.67	Sweden	0.60	United Kingdom	0.60
Spain	0.67	Switzerland	0.60	Australia	0.70
France	0.67	United States	0.60	Japan	0.70
United Kingdom	0.67	Germany	0.80	United States	0.90
Italy	0.67	France	0.80		
South Korea	0.67	Ireland	0.80		
Sweden	0.67	Italy	0.80		
Switzerland	0.67				
Ireland	1.00				
Netherlands	1.00				
United States	1.00				
Average	0.67	Average	0.60	Average	0.57

(table continues)

the list in 2014 that was in the same group in 2009. For the stability index, 2009 is used as the benchmark year because the billionaire group needs to be large enough in each year that the top 3, 5, or 10 exist. To be on the top 3 list, a country must have had at least 3 billionaires five years ago in order for the stability indicator to be measured. Similarly for top 5 and 10. There are thus more countries when stability is measured by the top 3 than by the top 5. There were too few billionaires in 2001 to calculate a stability index for most emerging-market countries. Low stability implies that new fortunes are coming on board often.

Table 8.3 shows stability rates by country. The data show much more dynamism in the South, where 47 to 57 percent on average of billionaires at the top remain unchanged. In contrast, the average in the North is 57 to 67 percent.

Among emerging economies, China and India show very different pictures. Despite similar population sizes, China is at the top of the list, indicating tremendous dynamism, while India is near or at the bottom. Both

Table 8.3   Five-year stability index for top 3, top 5, and top 10 billionaires, by country, 2009–14 *(continued)*

Top 3 country	Stability index	Top 5 country	Stability index	Top 10 country	Stability index
		Emerging economies			
China	0	China	0	Turkey	0.30
Kuwait	0	Brazil	0.40	Brazil	0.40
Russia	0	Russia	0.40	Russia	0.40
Chile	0.33	Turkey	0.40	Israel	0.50
United Arab Emirates	0.67	Hong Kong	0.60	Hong Kong	0.70
Brazil	0.67	Indonesia	0.60	India	0.70
Egypt	0.67	India	0.60		
Hong Kong	0.67	Israel	0.60		
Indonesia	0.67	Saudi Arabia	0.60		
India	0.67	Mexico	0.80		
Israel	0.67	Malaysia	1.00		
Mexico	0.67				
Malaysia	0.67				
Saudi Arabia	0.67				
Taiwan	0.67				
Thailand	0.67				
Turkey	0.67				
Ukraine	0.67				
South Africa	0.67				
Lebanon	1.00				
Average	0.57	Average	0.55	Average	0.47

Note: Stability is measured as the share of the top 3, 5, and 10 billionaires on the list in 2014 who were also in the top 3, 5, and 10 places in 2009.

Source: Author's calculations using data from Forbes, The World's Billionaires.

China and India have a handful of new-sector billionaires at the top, but India also has oil and steel fortunes, which are absent in China. Instead, China has billionaires who made their money in tradable goods, such as cars, appliances, and beverages. Of the top 10 billionaires in China, only 2 inherited their wealth, compared with half in India.

Takeaways

Five patterns emerge from this examination of changes in billionaire wealth. First, emerging-market billionaires tend to be younger than their advanced-country counterparts. Second, a wave of new businesses appeared in the early 1990s in the South, generating this pattern. A similar pattern exists for the new sectors in the North. Third, there is an up-or-out phenomenon among billionaires, especially in emerging markets: Fortunes grow rapidly or fall off the list. Fourth, there is more dynamism in the South than in the North. Finally, fortunes are not aging significantly in either the North or the South, indicating there is a lot of wealth creation as well as a lot of wealth destruction.

IV

INEQUALITY AND POLICY IMPLICATIONS

9

Inequality, Growth, and Redistribution

In December 2014, Heather Cho, vice president of Korean Air and daughter of the airline's chairman and chief executive, boarded a Korean Air flight in New York bound for Seoul. After she took her first-class seat, she was served macadamia nuts in a bag instead of the bowl she had expected. She called the cabin crew chief to her seat, berated him, allegedly made him kneel down, and then fired him. The plane returned to the gate for him to disembark, delaying the plane's departure over a bag of nuts. Korean Air tried to cover up the story, but the disgraced employee went to the press. Cho resigned from her post as vice president, apologized publicly, and spent four months in prison for violating aviation law.

"Nutgate" was only the latest in a series of scandals involving the Cho family. According to the *Washington Post*, "Heather Cho was criticized for giving birth to her twin boys in Hawaii, thus giving them US citizenship—meaning they could avoid Korea's mandatory military service. Cho's brother, Won-tae, was investigated by police for allegedly pushing an elderly woman in 2005. And Cho Yang-ho, their grandfather, was convicted of tax evasion in 2000."[1] Korean Air is now under scrutiny, as Heather Cho and her siblings compete to take control of the family business.

People love to hate the rich, and stories like this go viral because they justify such views. But these extreme cases are very rare. More common are

---

1. Adam Taylor, "Why 'Nut Rage' Is Such a Big Deal in South Korea," *Washington Post*, December 12, 2014.

the inheritors who live lavishly (but quietly) off their relative's earnings without playing an active role in the family business. But many inheritors also work extraordinarily hard to grow the family business. In Asia, the single-minded focus on company growth is why family control has worked so well for many enterprises, even as they pass from one generation to the next. These fast-growing companies in turn have been engines of job creation for their home country.

Consider the Tata Company. Ratan Tata joined Tata Sons in 1961 and quickly moved to a top management position. In 1991, when J. R. D. Tata stepped down as chairman, he named Ratan Tata his successor. The decision was derided, because the younger Tata was considered inexperienced and had been widely criticized for failures in running other parts of the business. Expectations were low about his ability to manage the growing business.

Ratan Tata surprised his critics, expanding the Tata Group by a factor of 40. By 2014 the company had annual revenue of more than $100 billion. Tata did not shy away from the increasing globalization that marked his term but faced it head on, with purchases of Tetley Tea and Jaguar Land Rover. He was innovative and took risks with the company, considering not only Western markets but the needs of the growing middle class in India (he was the force behind the Nano, India's fuel-efficient car, which sells for less than $3,000). Twice when he tried to retire, shareholders begged him to stay.

Problems arise when privileged sons and daughters behave more like Heather Cho and less like Ratan Tata. Cho is despised in Korea, viewed as a company brat who did not earn her position and exploited her power. Her birthright and behavior epitomize what people around the world dislike most about extreme wealth: that some individuals do not have to work hard, have it all, and treat others disrespectfully. In contrast, Ratan Tata is widely admired. Indeed, surveys[2] find him among the top 30 most admired people in the world. He was mocked when he took over Tata, but after he proved extraordinarily capable, views rapidly shifted.

The individuals who build large companies like Tata help countries modernize. Their successors are given the difficult task of growing market share and maintaining innovation in increasingly competitive markets. With well-established global brands, many emerging markets now face the challenge of ensuring that family ownership and management separate if and when company governance stops functioning. If companies do not

---

2. For example, YouGov, World's Most Admired 2014 poll, for the *Times of London*.

meet this challenge, emerging markets will face growing indignation at a wealthy class that does not expand companies and create jobs but enjoys privilege while the rest of the population stagnates.

For now, as this chapter demonstrates, a wealthy class that is growing faster than the rest of the population is primarily an advanced-country problem, not an immediate emerging-market concern. Wealth is growing rapidly in the South, but income is also growing rapidly. In contrast, the growth in extreme wealth in the North has coincided with stagnation of the rest.

Admiration of the Superrich in Emerging Markets

Ratan Tata is not the only billionaire that is widely admired. Many of the superrich are among the most admired people in the world. In 2014 Bill Gates, the richest person in the world, was also the most admired person in the world, followed by Barack Obama (number 2) and Vladimir Putin (number 3).[3] Although they are split over the type of political regime and ruler they admire, people uniformly appreciate a technology superstar and business tycoon. Warren Buffett and Hong Kong container mogul Li Ka-shing rank above the Dalai Lama, Lionel Messi, Angelina Jolie, and Angela Merkel. Other billionaires in the top 30 most admired people in the world include Oprah Winfrey and Ratan Tata. A clear split arises between individuals held in highest esteem by the populations of emerging markets and advanced countries. People in emerging markets have greater admiration for financial success and company building than do people in advanced countries. Bill Gates won in China hands down, with 19 percent of the vote, more than twice the 9 percent share runner-up President Xi Jinping of China received. While Gates made the top 10 list in all of the countries surveyed, he was among the top three in only five countries—all five of them emerging markets (China, Russia, Pakistan, Nigeria, and Egypt). None of the advanced countries—Australia, France, Germany, the United Kingdom, or the United States—put him (or any other billionaire) in the top three spots.

Inequality in the North and South

When asked how the government should address the wealth gap between the rich and the poor, people from the North and the South diverge. Emerging-market respondents favor growth and job creation, while advanced-country respondents prefer redistribution. A Pew poll asked what

---

3. "Bill Gates Is the Most Admired Person in the World," *YouGov*, January 10, 2014.

the best policy was to reduce the gap between rich and poor—high taxes on the wealthy and corporations to fund programs for the poor or low taxes to encourage investment and economic growth. In emerging markets low taxes to support growth received more votes. In advanced countries taxing the rich was the preferred response. Inequality has risen in some emerging markets and is a growing concern, but polls show that concerns about economic growth, price increases, and jobs in these countries far outweigh concerns over inequality.[4]

The difference likely reflects how conditions have changed over the past decade or so. Between 2006 and 2012, wealth grew faster in the South than the North. But GDP in the South grew even faster than wealth. In contrast, in the North extreme wealth grew three times faster than GDP (figure 9.1).[5]

Another way of viewing this evidence is through the inequality lens of Thomas Piketty, the author of *Capital in the Twenty-First Century*. Using data primarily from a few European countries and the United States, Piketty argues that in recent decades the return on capital (r) has been greater than the rate of economic growth (g). As a result of this one relationship ($r > g$) he argues that the wealthy, who benefit from interest income, saw and will continue to see their incomes grow faster than the incomes of the rest of the population, leading to an inexorable rise in income inequality.[6] Comparing growth in extreme wealth and country incomes, Piketty's formula is far more relevant to advanced countries than emerging econo-

---

4. *Emerging and Developing Economies Much More Optimistic than Rich Countries about the Future,* Pew Research Center, October 9, 2014.

5. Extreme wealth growth is calculated using all countries with at least 5 billionaires in 2006 and 2012. This sample includes 10 emerging markets and 11 advanced countries. The year 2006 was chosen as the base year in order to include China and Russia; results are similar if 1996 is used. 2012 was used as the end year because GDP data for 2013 (and 2014) were not available for the sample countries at the time of analysis. Wealth growth is calculated as the growth in wealth of the top 5 billionaires. The focus is on the top 5 billionaires in each period as the growth in wealth due to the rising number of billionaires is not calculable because initial wealth for this group is unobservable. Still, even using total wealth of billionaires from one period to the next to calculate growth (which vastly overestimates wealth growth because initial period wealth is counted as zero for new billionaires), wealth growth and income growth in emerging markets are roughly equal, and wealth grows more than three times faster than income in advanced countries.

6. Piketty's claim that $r > g$ is disputed by many economists because he does not account for diminishing returns to capital and his results include housing, which is subject to wide price swings. In fact, a survey of economists found that 80 percent of economists disagreed (Justin Wolfers, "Fellow Economists Express Skepticism About Thomas Piketty," *New York Times,* October 14, 2014).

Figure 9.1   Increase in wealth of the five richest people in each economy and increase in GDP, advanced countries and emerging economies, 2006–12

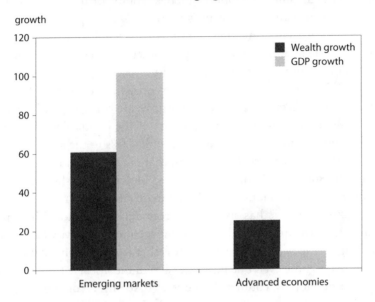

growth

Note: Figure is based on the change between 2006 and 2012 in the wealth of the five richest people in each economy in a balanced sample of economies with at least five billionaires. Sample comprises 10 emerging markets (Brazil, China, Hong Kong, India, Israel, Mexico, Malaysia, Russia, Saudi Arabia, and Turkey) and 11 advanced countries (Australia, Canada, France, Germany, Italy, Japan Spain, Sweden, Switzerland, the United Kingdom, and the United States).

Sources: Data from Forbes, The World's Billionaires; and World Bank, *World Development Indicators.*

mies. If the growth in wealth of an economy's richest individuals is taken as a broad measure of returns to capital (as shown in figure 9.1), it is indeed far greater than the GDP growth rate in advanced countries. While this evidence is consistent with $r > g$ for advanced countries, it does not show $r > g$ because growth in extreme wealth can be due to other things, like technology and innovation. But the evidence from emerging markets is not at all consistent with $r > g$, where GDP growth outpaces wealth growth.

The superstar theory highlights a redistribution of income toward the most talented people as a potential explanation for the rise in wealth (see chapter 1). In the superstar world, globalization and new technologies reorient income toward people of extreme ability and away from people of modest ability. The distribution of incomes—and as a result wealth—within a country becomes increasingly skewed. As economist Alfred Marshall (1890, 41) put it, "There never was a time at which a moderately good oil painting sold more cheaply than now, and...a first-rate painting sold so dearly."

The superstar story does not, however, appear to fit the developing world, where growth in extreme wealth has not been accompanied by a decline in the incomes of people of modest ability. Instead, the emergence of extreme wealth and mega firms is more likely to be part of a structural transformation that brings new employment opportunities and higher incomes to the majority of a country's workers. The creation of big firms and extreme wealth is part of development.

The different sources and economic consequences of extreme wealth in emerging markets and advanced countries are consistent with research on the rise in incomes of the vast majority of the population in emerging markets and the hollowing out of the middle class in the advanced countries over the past 20 years. To the extent that big money and large firms are helping the South modernize, broad-based income gains should accrue to developing countries along with the rise in extreme wealth.

Branko Milanović has spent his career examining global income inequality. He measures inequality in the most comprehensive way possible—by adding all the people in the world together (to the extent that there are data) and assigning everyone his or her actual income. He finds that most people in developing countries experienced strong income growth since 1990. As a result, for the world as a whole, inequality has declined markedly (Milanović 2005).

Figure 9.2 shows the income growth accruing to individuals in each segment of the global population. It reveals that most of the world's population (from the 10th to the 70th percentile) got richer over the past 20 years from 1988–2008. Most of this improvement took place in populous Asian countries, especially China. The dip after the 70th percentile reflects the stagnation of incomes of the majority in the advanced countries. This shift in the income distribution is consistent with one of the main findings of this book: that shifts in production, globalization, and wealth are benefiting workers in the South but not necessarily the North.

The spikes at either end of figure 9.2 show that the poorest did not share the large gains (far left) and that the richest saw rapid income growth (far right). The spike on the left is largely attributable to the lack of income convergence in the poorest countries, which failed to grow as rapidly as the average country, causing them to fall farther behind the rest. One explanation for this is that poverty may have a detrimental impact on growth, one that is more important than any potential impact of inequality (Ravallion 2012).

Surjit Bhalla (2002) was among the first to highlight the substantial reduction in global inequality as a result of high growth in poor countries,

Figure 9.2   Global income growth incidence curve, 1988–2008

income growth rate (percent)

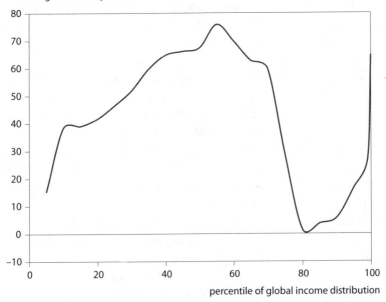

percentile of global income distribution

Source: Lakner and Milanović (2013).

dismissing the concept of divergence (in which poor countries grow slower than rich countries) popular at the time. He also noted a "political correctness" bias among a number of international organization officials who repeatedly expressed concern over the fact that poor countries are getting poorer and rich countries richer.

Although it is now widely recognized that global inequality has been declining, concern over rising within-country inequality has soared, with the top 1 percent or 0.1 percent considered the new boogeyman. Officials typically highlight US statistics and then generalize that rising inequality is one of the most serious economic problems of our time in nearly all countries. This pattern was evident in the "lifting the small boats" speech that International Monetary Fund (IMF) head Christine Lagarde made in Brussels in June 2015. Despite the title, which suggested a focus on the poor, the speech was largely about the superrich. Lagarde began the speech with indignation at the $1.3 billion income of the top hedge fund manager in 2014 and discussed increases in the shares of income and wealth going to the top 1 percent in the United States and other advanced countries. She then raised the concern that "economies like China and India seem to fit neatly into a traditional narrative which says that extreme inequality is an acceptable price to pay for economic growth."[7]

But is the extreme or growing inequality in China and India generated by a rise in the incomes of the superrich? Long time-series on the incomes for these countries are notoriously hard to come by. The World Top Incomes Database (Alvaredo et al. 2013b) includes data for China for 1986–2003. Although the share of the top 1 percent there rose during this period (from 2.7 to 5.9 percent), 5.9 percent remains a relatively low number—below the figure in Scandinavia. Data for India for 1985–99 show that the share of income of the top 1 percent rose from 8.2 to 9.0 percent. This 0.8 percentage point increase is not large and well within the margin of error, and 9 percent puts India in the range of Australia, Italy, and Japan. The average for the industrial countries in the World Top Incomes Database sample at the end of the period was about 10 percent.

It is in the Anglo countries that inequality driven by gains at the top is extreme: The share of income accruing to the top 1 percent exceeds 17 percent in the United States and 12 percent in Canada and the United Kingdom, all up significantly from about 8 percent in 1985. Enraged over the increasing concentration of income and wealth in the hands of the top 1 percent of the distribution, protestors in New York and London have chanted "we are the 99 percent," the slogan of the Occupy movement.

Figure 9.3 shows the share of the top 1 percent, 0.1 percent, and 0.01 percent of the income distribution in the United States as well as US billionaires' wealth as a percent of GDP. All four series increased, suggesting that both income and wealth are becoming more and more concentrated at the top in the United States and that the rest of the population is benefiting less from growth. The extraordinary rise in the standard of living of the 1 percent while the majority stagnates has shifted attention away from the low incomes of the poor to the extreme wealth of the few. However, in other countries it is the poor that are most in need of the world's attention.

Rising income inequality is a concern in the rich Anglo countries. For the world as a whole, however, income inequality has declined sharply, largely as a result of rapid economic growth in poor countries. China has contributed the most to both poverty reduction and extreme wealth in the South. Between the early 1990s and about 2013, it accounted for two-thirds of the reduction in global poverty measured as living below $1.25 a

7. Christine Lagarde, "Lifting the Small Boats," address at Les Grandes Conférences Catholiques, June 17, 2015.

Figure 9.3 Income shares of richest Americans, 1996–2012

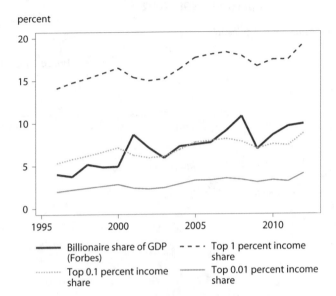

percent

Sources: Data from Forbes, The World's Billionaires; World Bank, *World Development Indicators*; and World Top Incomes Database (Alvaredo et al. 2013b).

day and nearly all the reduction in poverty measured at $2 a day.[8] China also accounted for more than a quarter of total billionaire creation in the South. The two phenomena represent two sides of the same modernization coin. In cross-country and time-series data, poverty reduction and billionaire creation are strongly correlated—not surprisingly, given that both are connected to growth in national income and trade, especially during periods of structural transformation. Concerns over rising inequality outside of the Anglo countries would do better to focus more on reducing poverty and less on the rise of the top.

Income Inequality versus Wealth Inequality

Income inequality and wealth inequality are not the same, although they are related. Because of very low levels of wealth at the bottom of the distribution and accumulation at the top, wealth tends to be even more skewed

---

8. Headcount data are not available for all years. So, data for 1990–96 are averaged and data for 2007–13 are averaged, to provide data for 89 countries with data in both periods.

Figure 9.4 Cross-country correlation between billionaire density and share of wealth owned by the top 1 percent, 1998–2002

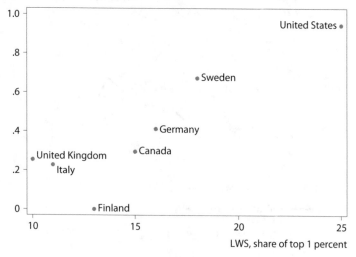

billionaires per million people

Sources: Data from Forbes, The World's Billionaires; and Luxembourg Wealth Survey (LWS).

than income.[9] The poorest people in terms of income tend to be the poorest in terms of wealth, but the reverse is not true—the wealthiest do not receive the highest incomes.

Cross-country data are harder to find on wealth inequality than income inequality, because wealth is more difficult to calculate. The Luxembourg Wealth Survey (LWS) provides data for a handful of countries, few of which have data that enable the share of wealth owned by the top 1 percent to be estimated. Using the LWS data, an Organization for Economic Cooperation and Development (OECD) study calculates the share of the top 1 percent in seven countries for various years between 1998 and 2002 (Jantti, Sierminska, and Smeeding 2008). The data on wealth concentration are highly correlated (correlation 0.89) with the density of billionaires in the population (figure 9.4). Billionaire density may thus be a reasonable proxy for wealth inequality across countries.

---

9. Below a certain income threshold, most income is spent on consumption, so wealth tends to be close to zero. In the United States, for example, the bottom 40 percent of the population controls just 0.2 percent of total wealth (Wolff 2010).

Figure 9.5   Cross-country correlation between billionaire density and share of income earned by the top 1 percent, 1996–2014

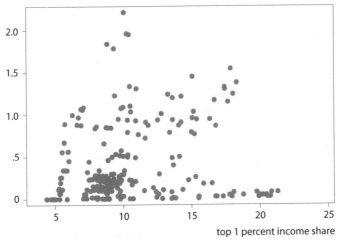

billionaires per million people

top 1 percent income share

Sources: Data from Forbes, The World's Billionaires; and World Top Incomes Database (Alvaredo et al. 2013b).

Extreme Wealth and Inequality

Wealth and income inequality are not closely related across countries or over time. Figure 9.5 shows the relationship between the Forbes measures of inequality (billionaire density), which tracks the LWS data closely, and the World Top Incomes Database income share of the top 1 percent for countries and years for which both series are available. Billionaire density and the World Top Incomes measures of income inequality are unrelated (correlation is below 0.10 and statistically insignificant). For the seven observations available, the World Top Incomes data are also not statistically significantly correlated with the LWS data. A high concentration of wealth does not appear to be closely correlated with a high share of income going to the top 1 percent.

Even if the cross-country correlation is low, it is possible that the series move together: In countries that have rising billionaire density, the share of national income earned by the top 1 percent may be rising. Figure 9.6 shows the relationship in annual changes. The correlation is close to zero: A rapidly growing billionaire population is not associated with a rising share of income by the top 1 percent.

Figure 9.6 Cross-country correlation between change in billionaire density and change in the share of income earned by the top 1 percent, 1996–2014

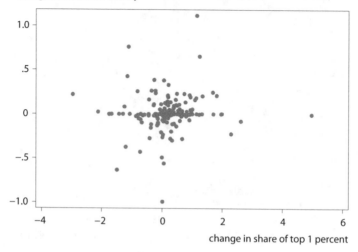

Sources: Data from Forbes, The World's Billionaires; and World Top Incomes Database (Alvaredo et al. 2013b).

Even within the United States, where wealth inequality and income inequality are accurately measured, the two series have not moved together in recent decades, according to Wojciech Kopczuk (2015), who analyzes a long time-series from a variety of data sources. He evaluates the share of wealth in the top 1 percent using a survey-based estimate, estate tax returns, and capital income from tax returns. Of these, only the capitalization measure shows a rise similar to that of income of the top 1 percent; the other two series are relatively flat. One explanation for the difference is that labor income has accounted for most of the rise in top incomes in the United States in recent decades. So, contrary to Piketty's focus on the returns to capital, income inequality is mostly explained by differences in salary/wage income. Income and wealth would move together only if capital income accounted for most of the change at the top of the distribution, but this does not appear to be the case.

The Superrich and Broader Inequality

The sharp decline in poverty coinciding with a large expansion in the population that is extremely wealthy in countries like China raises some questions: Does a larger number of superrich in a country affect broader

**Figure 9.7   Cross-country correlation between billionaire
density and income inequality, 1996–2012**

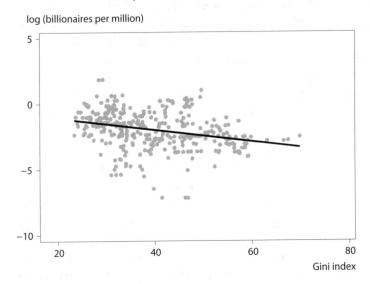

Sources: Billionaires: Forbes, The World's Billionaires; Gini index: Milanović (2014).

measures of income inequality? If the superrich reap rents that otherwise would accrue more broadly to the rest of the population as labor income, their rise would exacerbate inequality. If instead the superrich support growth and create jobs, their rise would reduce inequality.

Figure 9.7 presents a scatter diagram of inequality, using the most common measure (the Gini index) and the Forbes measures of inequality (billionaire density). The Gini index measures how far the income distribution in a country is from a distribution that is perfectly equal. A Gini of 0 implies perfect equality (everyone has equal wealth or income); a Gini of 100 represents perfect inequality (one person has all the wealth or income). If billionaires and inequality were closely connected, countries with a higher density of billionaires would have greater inequality. No such relationship is evident in figure 9.7. The correlation coefficient of billionaire density and the Gini is negative and statistically significant. Countries with more superrich have more, not less, equal income distributions.

The Arab Spring

At first blush the Arab Spring seems like a contradiction of the more sanguine view of extreme wealth in emerging markets. Protestors gathered in public squares chanting "bread, freedom, and social justice." To many, the demonstrations were evidence that resentment toward a rising economic elite was a catalyst of revolution. Dictators had ruled for decades, according to this view, but rising income and wealth inequality had reached a tipping point, which explained the timing of the revolt. In 2011 the *Financial Times* listed "significant inequality of wealth" as one of the major causes of the revolutions in Egypt and Tunisia.[10] A *New York Times* article comparing the London 2011 riots with the Arab Spring made income inequality a common theme, noting that "poverty and inequality helped fuel the revolution this winter in Egypt."[11] An article in *Foreign Policy* about the causes of the revolution argued that "income inequality has reached levels not before seen in Egypt's modern history."[12]

In fact, the levels of income and wealth inequality in Egypt and Tunisia are among the lowest in emerging markets (figure 9.8).[13] In both countries the major economic concern of the people was growth, job opportunities, and social mobility, not inequality. Their concerns are no surprise, given that unemployment in both countries, in the double digits, is among the highest in the world.

To the extent that the revolutions were about inequality, inequality of opportunity and access to legal and political systems were the main complaints. These issues are distinct from the anger in the United States over extravagant wages and bonuses to the elite in the private sector. Unemployed Egyptians and Tunisians are not queueing for private sector jobs but for safe government jobs that promise lifetime employment. The Egyptian and Tunisian governments, as well as others in the region, have

---

10. "Egyptian Fears," Lex Column, *Financial Times*, February 1, 2011.

11. David H. Kirkpatrick and Heba Afify, "For Egyptians, British Riots Are a Mix of Familiar and Peculiar," *New York Times*, August, 13, 2011.

12. Yasser El-Shimy, "Egypt's Struggle for Freedom," *Foreign Policy*, January 28, 2011.

13. A World Bank study explores inequality in Egypt to try to understand why perceptions of inequality and reality may differ. The authors review the evidence to identify potential problems with the data. They confirm that inequality in Egypt is low and find no evidence of a rise in income inequality before the revolution. Data on wealth are harder to find, but using data for 1950-79 on landholding, they show that the distribution became more equal over time, with some evidence of a reversal in the 1970s (Verme et al. 2014).

Figure 9.8 Inequality in selected emerging economies, 2000s

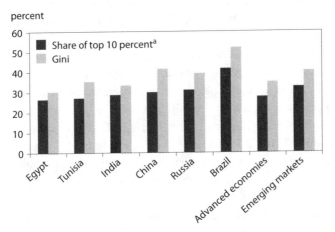

percent

Legend:
- Share of top 10 percent[a]
- Gini

a. Share of income captured by the top 10 percent of the population.
Source: Data from World Bank, *World Development Indicators*.

historically used civil service employment as part of the social safety net, with most citizens having at least one member of their extended family employed by the government. Over time this became fiscally unsustainable in all but the rich oil-exporting countries, and the failure of the government to absorb new members of the labor force was a cause for revolt. The private sector, however, has always been deemed a last resort, with workers preferring to wait for more respectable government jobs than work for a privately owned firm. Frustration in the Arab world has centered on governments' failed economic policies and political repression rather than the wealth of the 1 percent.

A key ingredient missing from the Middle East and North Africa has been dynamic entrepreneurs. It is the only emerging-market region in which this group is shrinking and inherited wealth is growing. Despite lower levels of inequality than the rest of the world, people in countries like Egypt and Tunisia feel the lack of opportunity more sharply, because the business sector is stagnating and income growth has been weak. Countries where rent seekers dominate the upper classes are not always the most statistically unequal countries in the world, because rent seekers typically do not accumulate nearly as much wealth as global innovators.

How Skewed Is the Wealth Distribution among Billionaires?

How has billionaire wealth changed over time in the North and the South? Has it become more skewed, with the richest individuals holding a larger share of wealth?

The share of the top 20 percent is a useful starting point. The 80–20 principle states that 80 percent of outcomes are attributable to 20 percent of causes. It holds for many phenomena: 80 percent of sales typically stem from 20 percent of customers, and 80 percent of market returns come from 20 percent of stocks. The economist Vilfredo Pareto uncovered this rule when he showed that 20 percent of the population held 80 percent of the land in his native Italy. A Pareto distribution is a skewed probability distribution used to describe many phenomena in economics, statistics, and business, as well as math and physics.

Not all so-called Pareto distributions produce the 80-20 split. For example, 20 percent of exporters account for more than 90 percent of exports on average in most countries (World Bank, Exporter Dynamics Database), revealing that exports are especially concentrated among the largest firms. The share of the top 20 percent is thus a good indicator of how concentrated a distribution is.

Using the Forbes billionaires data to calculate the share of billionaire wealth held by the top 20 percent of billionaires in a country (including all countries with at least five billionaires) reveals strong evidence of increasing skewedness of wealth everywhere. The magnitude of the increase is greater in the North, however.

In 1996, 20 percent of the billionaire population held about 40 percent of the extreme wealth in both the North and the South (table 9.1). By 2014 the top 20 percent held 57 percent of the wealth in the North and 51 percent in the South. In the United States, the richest 20 percent of billionaires owned 61 percent of all billionaire wealth. If these trends are common throughout the full wealth distribution, even for wealth below the billionaire threshold, then wealth in the North is becoming more heavily concentrated among the small percentage at the top. The richest of the rich are taking a larger and larger share of the pie.

Not only are there more billionaires but also individual billionaires are on average getting richer. Figure 9.9 shows the contribution of average individual billionaire wealth to growth in total billionaire wealth in the North and the South.[14] By construction the contribution of average wealth

---

14. Freund and Oliver (2016) provides details of the methodology.

Table 9.1 Share of wealth held by top 20 percent of billionaires in advanced countries and emerging economies, 1996–2014 (percent)

Year	Total	Advanced countries	Emerging economies
1996	40	41	40
2000	45	47	36
2005	50	50	47
2010	50	51	49
2014	55	57	51

Source: Author's calculations using data from Forbes, The World's Billionaires.

Figure 9.9 Contribution of intensive margin to annual growth of total real net worth of billionaires in advanced countries and emerging economies, 1996 and 2001–14

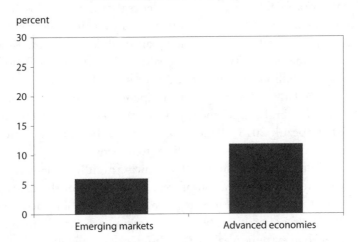

percent

Note: Intensive margin is the percent of total wealth growth that can be explained by increases in individual billionaire real net worth.

Source: Author's calculations using data from Forbes, The World's Billionaires.

and the number of billionaires sum to one. The extensive margin of wealth (the increase in the number of billionaires) explains the lion's share of the expansion in billionaire wealth in both the North and the South. But the intensive margin (the rise in average billionaire wealth) contributed more to rising wealth in the North than in the South: 12 percent of the rise in wealth in advanced countries is a result of richer billionaires, compared with 6 percent in emerging markets.[15] It is in the advanced countries that billionaires are on average getting richer over time.

Takeaways

President Obama called income inequality "the defining challenge of our time" and made it a focus of his second term. A recent OECD report warns that rising inequality will be "the major policy challenge for all countries." Even the IMF, whose core mandate is financial stability, put a new emphasis on income inequality, highlighting its deleterious effects on growth. Wall Street followed suit, with Standard and Poor's and Morgan Stanley issuing reports expressing concern over inequality. Oxfam went so far as to call for an end to extreme wealth by 2025, reversing levels to the 1990s.

Prioritizing reducing income and wealth inequality is problematic, for several reasons. First, wealth inequality and income inequality, used interchangeably by many policymakers, are different. The data on the distribution of wealth across the population are limited, but for the countries for which data are available, there is little evidence that wealth is closely related to income inequality, either across countries or over time. Sweden has low income inequality and high wealth inequality, while the United Kingdom had high income inequality and low wealth inequality. There is no correlation between billionaire density and the share of the top 1 percent in income. In the United States, growth in income inequality has not been associated with similar movements in wealth inequality, when carefully measured (Kopczuk 2015). Policymakers should be more specific when discussing inequality, because the policies to remedy each may be different.

Second, although extreme wealth is growing rapidly in many countries, the increase in the concentration of wealth at the top of the distribution while the rest of population stagnates is largely an advanced-country (especially Anglo-country) problem: In emerging economies, incomes are rising faster than extreme wealth. This difference may explain why it is the rich countries where the population is calling for more equitable distribution while populations in the South remain more concerned about economic growth and jobs. Reducing poverty and increasing opportunity,

---

15. If only individuals who were billionaires in 1996 dollars are included, the intensive margin is larger, but the difference between the North and the South remains. Using this cutoff, the intensive margin is 20 percent in the North and 14 percent in the South.

not the rise of the top 1 percent, are the most important considerations in emerging markets.

Third, the focus on income inequality and wealth inequality, especially the share of the top 1 percent, as a major global concern reflects a US or Anglo bias. Global inequality has declined, as developing countries have been growing faster than industrial countries. This outcome is very big news and should be celebrated and made as well known as concerns about inequality in Anglo countries. Even within advanced countries, evidence that the top 1 percent is earning more and getting richer is limited to a handful of countries. In most of the world, the focus should be on the other end of the distribution: raising the incomes of the very poor.

To the extent that growth in extreme wealth corresponds to the rise of emerging-market multinationals, it is a sign of health in emerging markets. As shown in previous chapters, extreme wealth and development are linked. In countries undergoing structural transformation, a growing number of company founders is a positive sign. Wealth accrues to the creators of the large companies that move people out of agriculture and into modern production. It is only when wealth is growing primarily in the rent-driven and internally oriented sectors that it is problematic in emerging markets. When it is, wealth at the top is unlikely to grow as rapidly. In most fast-growing emerging markets, it is the group of company founders that is growing most rapidly.

The process is different in advanced countries, where growth in extreme wealth is more likely to be associated with services and technology and therefore has a more ambiguous effect on job opportunities facing the average worker. Advanced countries have also seen extreme wealth grow much faster than income. Wealth is increasingly skewed in the North, helping explain why there is more pushback against the superrich there.

10

Policies for Promoting Innovation and Equity

How far should the government go to foster big business in developing economies? Development institutions such as the World Bank urge governments to focus on securing property rights, ensuring the free entry and exit of firms, and opening up to trade and foreign investment. These features are important for creating an atmosphere in which businesses can grow. But in developing economies, reform can move slowly, access to finance is limited, and uncertainties abound. Should governments there do more to promote transformative, large-scale entrepreneurship?

This chapter begins with the most basic mechanisms for efficient resource allocation: property rights, free entry, and openness to trade and investment. It then discusses the potential for promoting entrepreneurship to spur modernization. The intuition from firm-level research is that success involves facilitating the development of large enterprise and forcing firms to compete globally. The chapter also discusses ways to reduce wealth that is not associated with entrepreneurial talent.

Creating an Environment that Is Conducive to Growth

Resources flow to the most productive uses when commerce is encouraged. William Baumol (1990) underscores the importance of creating rules that incentivize productive activity. He shows that in ancient Rome, productive enterprise was not well rewarded and technology did not spread. The water mill, for example, was developed in the 1st century BC but was little used then, except occasionally to mill grain. Under the Sung Dynasty in

China (960–1270), all property belonged to monarchs, and wealth and prestige were reserved for people who studied Confucian philosophy and calligraphy. Innovations in paper, printing, the compass, waterwheels, water clocks, and gun powder occurred during this period, but the absence of property rights hindered the spread of industry based on these major discoveries. In contrast, during the High Middle Ages and the 18th century Industrial Revolution, entrepreneurship was well rewarded; in both periods innovation spread rapidly. Using these and other historical examples, Baumol argues that when the rules of the game favor entrepreneurship, it flourishes; when they do not, even great ideas do not spread.

Kevin Murphy, Andrei Shleifer, and Robert Vishny (1991) develop a theoretical model that identifies the three main factors that make entrepreneurship, as opposed to rent seeking or other less socially valuable choices, more attractive: property rights, firm entry, and openness to trade. Property rights allow people to build their companies without fear of expropriation.[1] Easy entry and expansion of firms allow talented people to create firms and grow them quickly. Trade provides a large market for goods and ensures that price incentives are correct, guiding resources to their most productive uses. Business turnover and trade ensure that entrepreneurs compete in contestable markets. They are precisely the ingredients that are coming together in the developing countries where company founders are thriving and commerce is growing rapidly.

Ensuring Ease of Entry

Hernando de Soto demonstrated the onerous nature of business regulations in Peru. In 1983 his research team tried to establish a garment factory in Lima. After 289 days, 11 requirements, and direct costs 31 times the average monthly wage, they succeeded (Clilft 2003). De Soto (1989) attributes the prevalence of informal businesses in Peru to excessive regulation. Businesses stay small and informal because becoming big is very costly. As a result they lack access to capital, and markets remain uncompetitive. The high cost of regulation partly explains why it took so long for emerging markets to begin producing the mega firms that succeed on global markets.

The World Bank's Doing Business project is built on de Soto's work. Doing Business indicators provide a means to compare business regulations across countries. The first indicator developed was ease of business entry, which measures how long it takes to register a typical business.

---

1. The importance of property rights in promoting entrepreneurship and commerce is well known. It is therefore discussed here only briefly.

Research using the data shows that countries in which business entry is easier have less corruption and tend to be richer (Djankov et al. 2002).

Ease of business entry ensures that the most productive firms are in the market. Lean regulation also prevents government bureaucrats and intermediaries from extracting rents. When regulation is burdensome, requiring complex paperwork and approvals, government officials can solicit bribes to smooth the process, and intermediaries who understand the business can flourish.

Brazil is known for excessive regulation, though in recent years conditions have been improving. In 2005, according to Doing Business indicators, it took 152 days to start a business, more than three times as long as in China or Russia and twice as long as in India. Brazilians use the word *despachante* (meaning customs agent or dispatcher) to refer to the intermediaries who flourish when regulations are excessively complex. Their prominence is revealed in John Grisham's 1999 novel *The Testament* (p. 376):

> The *despachante* is an integral part of Brazilian life. No business, bank, law firm, medical group, or person with money can operate without the services of a *despachante*. He is a facilitator extraordinaire. In a country where the bureaucracy is sprawling and antiquated, the *despachante* is the guy who knows the city clerks, the courthouse crowd, the bureaucrats, the customs agents. He knows the system and how to grease it. No official paper or document is obtained in Brazil without waiting in long lines, and the *despachante* is the guy who'll stand there for you. For a small fee, he'll wait eight hours to renew your auto inspection, then affix it to your windshield while you're busy at the office. He'll do your voting, banking, packaging, mailing—the list has no end.

Excessive regulations create delays and impose extra costs on businesses. They also divert resources into unproductive activities like those performed by *despachantes*.

Brazil has improved its Doing Business indicators, reducing the number of days required to start a business by almost half since 2005. It is replacing business registration and customs bureaucracies with electronic one-stop shops. The great advantage that new technology brings is that it is not corruptible. Getting rid of excessive bureaucracy in busines entry is an important step in development, because it facilitates business development and expansion and helps direct talent to more productive uses.

Opening Up to Trade

Entrepreneurs can build mega firms only if the market for their product is large. Small countries need trade to reach such markets; the growth of a company that exports is not constrained by country size. Openness also allows companies to access inputs needed for production.

Beyond providing a large market, openness to trade ensures that price incentives are correct, steering firms to produce the most competitive products. When tariffs are high, it becomes more profitable to produce import-competing goods than exported goods, despite the fact that producing such goods does not represent the best use of a country's resources. The nearly 800 percent tariff on imported rice in Japan is an extreme example of how protection directs production to goods that are not aligned with a country's comparative advantage.

The growth literature shows an additional benefit from jointly pursuing ease of business entry and trade liberalization. When economists examine which countries have benefited from increasing trade they find that trade leads to a higher standard of living in flexible economies but not in rigid economies (Freund and Bolaky 2008; Chang, Kaltani, and Loayza 2009). The intuition is that trade provides the right price signals for the best businesses to grow but that ease of entry and exit are important for resource reallocation to actually happen. If there are constraints on business creation, superstar firms may never be born. Analysis shows that business regulation, especially on firm entry, is more important than financial development, higher education, or rule of law as a complementary policy to trade liberalization. After controlling for the standard determinants of per capita income, a 1 percent increase in trade is associated with more than a 0.5 percent rise in per capita income in economies that facilitate firm entry but has no positive income effects in more rigid economies (Freund and Bolaky 2009). The findings support firm-level studies showing that the beneficial effects of trade liberalization result largely from moving resources to the most productive firms. If new firms cannot enter and the best firms cannot grow, the gains from trade are largely absent.

Undervaluing the Exchange Rate

The real exchange rate is a critical price determining global competitiveness and hence a complement to open trade policies. It is a measure of the ratio of domestic costs to foreign costs, using the same basket of goods in the same currency.[2] Preventing overvaluation is important because it pushes resources toward the nontradable sectors as tradables become less

---

2. For example, the *Economist*'s Big Mac index measures the relative cost of a Big Mac in different countries. When the index diverges significantly in countries at similar stages of development, the home currency of the more expensive hamburger is very likely overvalued.

competitive: Imports will outperform domestically produced competing goods, and exports will become costly abroad. Given that nontradables are produced in inherently less contestable markets, such an outcome is bad for development. It prevents the most productive firms from growing through foreign markets. A large and growing body of evidence finds that an undervalued real exchange rate helps countries grow precisely because it pushes resources into the tradable sector (Hausmann, Prichett, and Rodrik 2005; Jones and Olken 2008; Bhalla 2012; Freund and Pierola 2012).

Profiting from Foreign Direct Investment

Another way to move resources to their most efficient uses and develop large firms rapidly is through foreign direct investment (FDI). Singapore used this strategy effectively, as noted in chapter 4. Foreign firms invested in the country to take advantage of low labor costs and a relatively good business climate, and a domestic logistics industry developed around the growing manufacturing sector. Singapore remains a hub for foreign investment, but it has also developed its own multinationals. China's development strategy has also benefited from large joint ventures with foreign firms, which raised productivity, revealed China's potential for trade, and highlighted the importance of global supply chains.

Attracting the largest multinationals can have important aggregate effects. Many of the top exporters in a typical developing country are foreign multinationals. For years Costa Rica's top exporter was Intel.[3] Vietnam's leading exporter is Samsung. These large firms require inputs and logistics; demand by them improves the business climate. The success of one large multinational attracts other multinationals, further improving resource allocation. After Intel's arrival in Costa Rica, for example, companies such as Infosys and Hewlett-Packard moved in. Big investors like Texas Instruments, Motorola, and HP helped Bangalore, India, develop. The region later created blockbuster technology firms of its own, such as Infosys and Wipro.

A growing body of literature shows that FDI has positive effects on domestic business. Spillovers to firms in the same industry have been hard to find, but evidence shows strong positive effects on upstream industries in the home country (Javorcik 2004, Blalock and Gertler 2008). Foreign firms require high-quality inputs; to obtain them, they help local suppliers upgrade their products. Foreign-owned firms also teach domestic firms

---

3. Intel closed its Costa Rican factory in 2014 and moved its operations to Malaysia.

how to trade. Former managers with knowledge of global markets may start their own companies, or the foreign firm's success may provide information to domestic businesses about the value of trade. In Mexico, for example, proximity to multinational firms increased Mexican firms' likelihood of becoming exporters (Aitken, Hanson, and Harrison 1997).

In order for FDI to spur development, markets must be competitive. When foreign businesses are profitable because of market barriers, they may seek to maintain or expand them, hurting growth. In contrast, when foreign firms take advantage of resource endowments in a competitive market, they use resources more effectively. Theodore Moran (2011) finds that the extent of competition in the market in which the investment occurs is the most important factor in determining how positive the effect of FDI is.

Adopting Industrial Policy that Promotes Large-Scale Entrepreneurship

A good business climate is necessary for business to flourish, but it may not be sufficient, especially in a world of large enterprises, which require substantial financing. Large US steel and rail companies developed with government subsidies; major Japanese car companies grew under family control, with financing from their own banks sanctioned by the government.

In the most rapid recent industrializers, the state was heavily involved in both running enterprises and promoting large-scale entrepreneurship. In Korea the *chaebol*-controlled firms began their ascent in the 1960s and 1970s, with assistance from special tax treatment and low-interest loans. The export promotion policies of President Park Chung-hee shaped the global footprint of firms like Samsung, LG, and Hyundai. "Mammoth enterprise—considered indispensable, at the moment, to our country—plays not only a decisive role in the economic development and elevation of living standards," wrote Park, "but further, brings about changes in the structure of society and the economy" (Park 1962, 228–29). These firms undeniably helped Korea develop: Today Samsung alone accounts for about 20 percent of the Korean economy.

Following the success of Korea and the other Asian Tigers with industrial policy and export-led growth, Latin American governments experimented with export-promotion policies in recent decades. Their efforts were mostly on a small scale, targeting many firms with tax incentives and cheap loans. To promote nontraditional exports, for example, the Dominican Republic experimented with subsidized government loans of up to $500,000; Costa Rica offered tax credits to exporters of nontraditional goods. These programs enjoyed modest success, but they failed to generate the kind of large-scale entrepreneurship that transforms an economy. Why were export-oriented industrial policies in Japan, Korea, and Taiwan successful while attempts in much of the rest of the world were not?

Korea's program involved three important features: export orientation, competition between large enterprises to receive benefits, and withdrawal of benefits when firms did not perform. Small domestic markets, which tend to have oligopolies, do not provide a good playing field on which to evaluate firm performance. Competing in foreign markets is a better gauge and provides companies with the demand needed for rapid growth.

External orientation is not sufficient, however; privately owned firms must compete and operate on a large enough scale to matter to the economy. Korea's policy targeted not just the industry but also the firm. Global targets forced firms to compete for privileges, allowing only the best to grow rapidly.

The economic intuition behind industrial policy (defined as the government's use of economic incentives to promote a particular sector) is that it compensates for a market distortion that prevents the optimal amount of investment, given social returns. Hefty initial investments and early losses may deter private investment, especially when access to finance is limited or other firms can learn from the first investor about a product's marketability with smaller startup costs later, reducing future profitability of the pioneer. Production may be associated with learning externalities that firms do not internalize. For example, a manufacturer may benefit from improved production techniques and less waste over time, but not realize this before undertaking investment. A few large firms may need to be active in a sector or a region in order to make production and exporting profitable, because of logistics or upstream linkages. Under any of these conditions, the government may need to provide a push to get an industry started.

Economists have long recognized the theoretical possibility that market distortions exist that industrial policy could remedy, but most are skeptical about industrial policy working in practice, because of three main concerns: (1) governments are not good at "picking winners"; (2) the appropriate intervention (taxes or subsidies) depends on market structure and the nature of distortion, which varies by industry and can be difficult to identify; and (3) the process is highly corruptible, because choosing recipients is political. Resources are likely to flow to the best-connected sectors and firms rather than the most productive ones, while unproductive intermediaries and government officials enrich themselves at taxpayers' expense. The cure may be worse than the disease.

An ongoing attempt at government-promoted private enterprise in Russia highlights these concerns. In 2009 President Dmitry Medvedev dreamed up the Skolkovo Innovation Center as Russia's answer to Silicon Valley. The government spent more than $2 billion building a domestic high-tech sector, which it located in the neighborhood of Russia's super-rich to garner private sector support. So far the new center is providing high returns—albeit not of the kind planned. The innovation center's figureheads were arrested on embezzlement charges in April 2013 and soon thereafter President Vladimir Putin reversed the tax and planning benefits offered to investors.[4] As a result none of the large-scale investments ever materialized. Lack of transparency in government regulation and procurement has continued to skew incentives away from productive business development toward rent taking. A Korean-style model of competition for financing, using a metric that can be objectively measured, is needed.

Supporting Firms Rather than Sectors

Much industrial policy—especially failed policy—has focused on industries (often import-competing instead of export-oriented). The importance of large-scale entrepreneurship points to the potential usefulness of supporting firms as opposed to sectors. The government need not pick winners, international competition can do that, ensuring that financing goes to the right firms and graft is reduced.

Industrial policies that have succeeded in creating global firms and starting new industries share three important features. First, they encourage investment in the export sector. Second, rather than spreading money across a swath of firms, they target a few private domestic firms that compete for financing with other domestic firms by showing export success. Third, the government must be capable of running a fair contest among firms. Because it is very easy to hijack competition in a nontransparent system, countable output metrics (such as export targets and production growth) rather than input measures (such as research and development or hiring) should be used. Korea used bills of lading from the port to measure firms' exports in the 1960s and 1970s, precisely because these documents could not be falsified.

One example of (eventual) success with this kind of industrial policy comes from Latin America. In 1969 the Brazilian government founded aircraft maker Embraer. As a state-owned enterprise, Embraer was a huge failure, with losses running into the hundreds of millions of dollars in

---

4. Alec Luhn, "Not Just Oil and Oligarchs," *Slate Magazine*, December 9, 2013.

the 1980s. To try to turn these mammoth government expenditures into revenues, the government privatized Embraer in 1994, but the firm continued to receive concessional financing. Júlio Bozano (now a billionaire) and his bank led the consortium of investors. They installed a business guru, Mauricio Botelho, with no aircraft experience, as CEO. Backed by a strong board, Botelho completely changed the company's course. When it was privatized, Embraer was a mess, involved in a number of losing product lines. Botelho dropped all projects but one, the 50-seater jet. The move represented a big risk at the time, given the commanding position of the Canadian company Bombardier in this market. Following deep restructuring and concessional financing by the government, Embraer soon became highly profitable. Its success was solidified when it became globally competitive in the mid-1990s. Embraer now leads the regional jet market, with technology that Bombardier cannot match.[5] "This is an example of how a strategy can make a company a success—or kill it if the strategy is wrong," notes Botelho.[6] External orientation, private enterprise, and scale all came together in Embraer, now a $5 billion company.

The Brazilian government's financing was not as explicitly competitive as the Korean government's was. Instead, large-scale private investors monitored the firm's performance.

Identifying Market Distortion

One reason why highly productive firms may need government assistance to finance large investments is that financial systems are weak: Bank financing is unavailable (because property rights laws and credit registries are not in place) and stock markets are not developed. The legal environment for future earnings–based bank financing and stock market development is significantly weaker in developing countries than in advanced countries (LaPorta et al. 1997, Djankov, McLiesh, and Shleifer 2007, among many others). The absence of developed capital markets prevents high-performing firms in emerging markets from growing at their potential and expanding rapidly in foreign markets.[7]

---

5. Christiana Sciaudone, "Embraer Seen Winning Regional-Jet Contest with Bombardier," *Bloomberg Business*, November 7, 2013.

6. Russ Mitchell, "The Little Aircraft Company That Could," *Fortune*, November 15, 2005.

7. Some firms from developing countries have tried to tap financial markets abroad, mainly through listings on the New York, London, or Hong Kong exchanges. But these firms are already very large, and they are typically energy companies or other resource-oriented concerns, or in communications or financial services, such as telecom or banks.

Using a dataset of listed firms from 51 countries, Tatiana Didier, Ross Levine, and Sergio Schmukler (2014) show that in a typical country only a few of the largest firms issue securities. Firms that issue bonds or equity grow much faster than nonissuers. They find that in developed economies small issuers grow faster than large issuers, suggesting that small firms are most constrained. In contrast, in developing economies large issuers grow the fastest, suggesting that credit constraints are much broader and may disproportionately constrain the largest firms.

In most developing countries, equity and bond markets are underdeveloped, preventing firms from growing to potential. This finding dovetails with the literature on firm dynamics (discussed in chapter 3), which shows that the failure of the best firms to grow large over time constrains growth in developing countries. Government-supported financing and tax incentives can help firms with the potential to become large multinationals grow faster in emerging markets. It is, however, important that such policies be limited to additive financing (not financing that crowds out the private banking sector) and that they be phased out once a country develops a financial system capable of intermediating funds.

Limiting Unproductive but Profitable Activities

In addition to promoting entrepreneurship, government policy can reduce the extent to which resources go to activities that do little to boost (or actually reduce) aggregate welfare. Countries with sizable shares of inherited and financial sector wealth may be justified in taxing them.

Raising or Imposing Estate Taxes

Many countries apply estate and inheritance taxes on large transfers in order to mitigate the concentration of wealth.[8] These taxes exempt the vast majority of wealth. In the United States, for example, the estate tax of 40 percent is charged only on estates above $5.43 million per individual, and only the amount by which the estate exceeds the exemption is taxed. In Korea a progressive inheritance tax ranges from 10 to 50 percent for net worth above 3 billion Korean won (about $2.55 million). In 2015 Japan raised its maximum rate from 50 to 55 percent and expanded the base.

---

8. Estate taxes are applied to the combined estate of the deceased. Inheritance taxes are applied to each recipient's portion. Estate taxes are typically coupled with gift taxes, in order to ensure that the transfer of assets before death is treated the same way as the transfer after death.

Whether or not taxing inheritance makes economic sense depends on whether it distorts the productive behavior of the bestower. Opponents of estate tax argue that it discourages entrepreneurs from expanding their companies, because a central motive behind acquiring wealth is the desire to leave it to one's heirs. They also worry that companies may be divided upon the death of the founder if their heirs do not have enough money to pay taxes and run the business. Estate tax might also encourage companies to move to lower tax jurisdictions or engage in costly and unproductive tax avoidance.

The first two concerns are largely theoretical. There is little evidence that bequests are at the top of founders' minds. Indeed, Wojciech Kopczuk (2007) finds that much of estate planning among the wealthy elderly takes place only after the onset of a serious illness. Even if founders are considering succession plans, company leaders may actually work harder in the presence of an estate tax in order to leave a greater after-tax business to their children.

The evidence that the exclusion level for estate taxes greatly affects small businesses is weak. Donald Bruce and Mohammed Moshin (2006) find no significant effect of the US estate tax exclusion policy in effect from 1983 to 1998 on entrepreneurial activity, despite the comparatively low exclusion level of $750,000.

On the last concern, a host of resource needs, logistics requirements, lifestyle choices, and other tax considerations affect the choice of a company's location. Research suggests that to the extent taxes matter for location, corporate taxes are much more important than estate taxes in affecting the location choice, and corporate taxes matter for the parent more than subsidiaries (see, for example, Markle and Shackelford 2012). Bermuda is a tax haven because it has no corporate tax, not because it allows wealthy people to avoid estate taxes. A moderate estate tax is unlikely to be a critical decision in where to locate business or where the wealthy choose to reside.

Estate taxes could actually have a positive effect, by encouraging heirs to work harder. As Andrew Carnegie famously said, "The parent who leaves his son enormous wealth generally deadens the talents and energies of the son and tempts him to lead a less useful and less worthy life than he otherwise would" (Carnegie 1891, 1962, A1). Douglas Holtz-Eakin, David Joulfaian, and Harvey Rosen (1993) offer empirical support for this conjecture. They use US tax return data from 1982 and 1983 and find that individuals who receive larger inheritances are significantly more likely to leave the labor force.

Figure 10.1   Correlation between per capita GDP and estate tax rate, 2013

estate tax rate

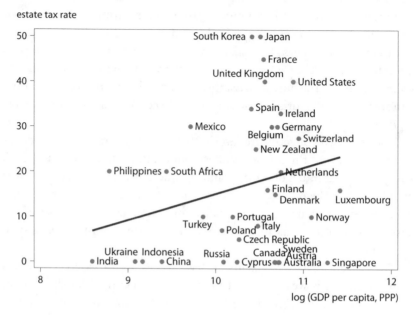

log (GDP per capita, PPP)

PPP = purchasing power parity

Sources: Data from World Bank, *World Development Indicators;* and EY International Estate and Inheritance Tax Guide 2013.

The estate tax can be an important source of revenue and redistribution. In the United States, both the tax and the tax base declined substantially in the 2000s. In 2001 estate tax was imposed on estates greater than $675,000, at a rate of 55 percent; in 2015 the tax was imposed only on estates that exceeded $5.43 million, and the rate was 40 percent. As a result of changes in the law, nominal estate tax revenues fell from $216 billion in 2001 to $48 billion in 2011. (To put these figures in context, in 2001 estate tax revenue could have covered the cost of the food stamp program 14 times over. In 2011 the revenue could have covered just two-thirds of the program.[9])

Estate taxes around the world vary significantly (figure 10.1). Although not all developed countries have high estate taxes (many rich countries, including Sweden and Singapore, have no estate tax at all), all of the coun-

---

9. The United States spent $15.5 billion on food stamps in 2001 and $71.8 billion 2011 ("Supplemental Nutrition Assistance Program Participation and Costs," US Department of Agriculture, August 7, 2015, www.fns.usda.gov/sites/default/files/pd/SNAPsummary.pdf).

Figure 10.2 Correlation between share of billionaire wealth in advanced countries that is inherited and share of total tax revenue from legacy taxes

share of billionaire wealth that is inherited, 2014 (percent)

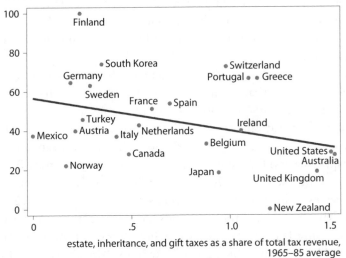

estate, inheritance, and gift taxes as a share of total tax revenue, 1965–85 average

Sources: Data from Forbes, The World's Billionaires; and OECD revenue statistics database.

tries with high estate taxes are developed countries. Many developed countries have low estate taxes.

Figure 10.2 shows estate tax as a share of total tax revenue and the share of inherited billionaires in the North. It suggests that the advanced countries that have historically relied more heavily on estate taxes for revenue have managed to limit inherited wealth.

Estate Taxes Promote Philanthropy

A potential additional benefit of estate taxes is that they encourage philanthropy, as the wealthy seek to reduce the value of an estate before it is transferred. Frank Doti (2003) uses variation in US estate tax law to estimate the effect of taxes on philanthropy. The estate tax law of 1917 did not allow for deduction of charitable bequests. This oversight was rectified in 1921 (retroactive to 1918). Doti finds that between 1917 and 1921 gross estates increased 25 percent and charitable bequests increased 3,419 percent, which is more than 34 times the charitable bequests reported at the beginning of the period. His finding suggests that high tax rates encourage the wealthy to leave a larger share of their estates to charity.

The 19th century US industrialists were major philanthropists during their lifetimes. Their behavior may have been related to taxation, as well as the desire to leave a legacy. The federal estate tax was first introduced in the mid-1800s, but it was low (West 1980). It reached a temporary peak of 15 percent in 1902 before being repealed until 1916, when modern estate tax was enacted.[10] It rose rapidly every few years, from 10 percent in 1916 to 25 percent in 1917, hitting 77 percent by 1941. Corporate and income taxes also rose.

The value of philanthropy in development is hard to quantify, but anecdotal evidence shows that it is important and, to the extent that estate taxes encourage it, that is an additional benefit of such taxes. Andrew Carnegie is probably the world's best-known philanthropist. He died in 1919, when estate taxes were 25 percent and the maximum income tax rate was 73 percent. His foundation built more than 2,500 libraries. One study finds that the return on these libraries is six to one: For every $1 a city puts in, the library creates $6 in social return (Carnegie Library of Pittsburgh 2005). At least 6 of the 28 so-called robber barons are associated with major universities, including Leland Stanford, Cornelius Vanderbilt, Andrew Carnegie (Carnegie-Mellon), James Buchanan Duke (Duke University), and John D. Rockefeller and Marshall Field (University of Chicago). Two large foundations, Carnegie and Rockefeller, support development to this day.

The superrich of the 1950s also gave heavily to charity, in part because US estate taxes reached nearly 80 percent. James Chapman, an oil baron, left his $100 million fortune to universities (mainly the University of Tulsa) and medical institutions, leaving little more than their home to his wife and son. Hugh Roy Cullen, another oil man, left $30 million to the University of Houston and at least $20 million to hospitals. Amon Carter used his oil wealth to promote aviation, starting American Airlines. He put half his wealth into a charitable foundation (Lundberg 1968).

Historical examples of large-scale philanthropy in Europe are rarer, likely related to nominal inheritance or estate taxes on close relatives. The imperial inheritance tax in Germany, imposed in 1906, exempted children and other direct descendants. The French had a maximum rate of 5 percent for children. The British Empire set a maximum estate tax rate of 8 percent until 1907, when it was increased to 15 percent. The cantons of Switzerland, among the first to establish an inheritance tax in Europe, set maximum rates for immediate family below 3 percent.[11]

---

10. Most states charged estate taxes even during the period of appeal.

11. See West (1980) for a history of inheritance and estate taxes.

Emerging markets have yet to see the kind of large-scale philanthropy that existed in the United States in the early 1900s, possibly because of low estate taxes, the novelty of extreme wealth, or cultural differences. There are signs of change, however, especially among billionaires who emigrated to countries with a tradition of philanthropy.

Among the most notable is George Soros, a native Hungarian and US citizen who has given an estimated $8 billion toward promoting liberalism, education, and democracy in Eastern Europe. Mo Ibrahim, a British citizen born in Sudan, created the Mo Ibrahim Prize for Achievement in African Leadership, which offers $5 million to leaders who help their countries escape war, democratize, and prosper. He has also joined the Giving Pledge, a commitment by the world's wealthiest individuals and families to dedicate the majority of their wealth to philanthropy. Leonard Blavatnik, a US citizen born in the Soviet Union, donated $117 million to Oxford University to establish the Blavatnik School of Government there.

Russia has experienced recent growth in philanthropy. Ruben Vardanian (whose net worth is estimated at $850 million) ran the investment bank Troika for more than a decade before selling it. He now devotes his money and energy to charity, focusing on education, infrastructure, and renovating archeological sites. He does not consider it philanthropy. "Philanthropy usually means you're giving money and forgetting about it. I am quite actively involved in the management decisions. It's like capitalism... Keeping all this pressure, being a tough investment banker, but delivering results for charities."[12] His children will inherit only property, no money. According to the Foundation Center, by the end of 2006 wealthy Russians had established more than 20 foundations (Spero 2014). Some of Russia's biggest philanthropists have preferred to donate outside the country.

China, Brazil, and India have also witnessed a flurry of activity in recent years. Wealth-X reports the top five philanthropist countries in three categories: the most generous, most numerous, and most frequent. The United States tops the list in all three, but China places third on most numerous, India ranks second on most generous (with China fourth), and Singapore comes in third on most frequent (with China fifth). Emerging-market countries take one-third of the spots. The self-made superrich make up a larger share of philanthropists than people who inherited their fortunes. Education is the top philanthropic priority.

---

12. "Ruben Vardanian, Former Troika Dialog CEO: A Grumbling Optimist," The Monday Interview, *Financial Times*, January 4, 2015.

Philanthropy is also spreading to smaller countries. The richest man in the Czech Republic, Petr Kellner, supports education, especially of low-income children. His foundation, Open Gate, provides about $5 million a year.

Wealthy foundations tend to have different (sometimes complementary) goals from the government.[13] Philanthropy disproportionately targets education, for example, while governments spend relatively more on the social safety net.

In many countries, charities may be more efficiently run than government funds. As Andrew Carnegie claimed, the wealthy are better managers of capital than governments. To the extent that the estate tax deduction encourages philanthropy, it creates more aggregate revenue for charities and government spending combined.

Taxing Unproductive Activities

Another large group of superrich that is of growing concern are financial sector billionaires. Some financial activities are likely to be unproductive from a social standpoint, especially compared with engineering or computer science. Because they offer high returns, they attract top talent.

Studies of the United States find that the most talented individuals are diverted from innovative sectors because of the large personal economic gains associated with the financial sector. Thomas Philippon and Ariell Reshef (2009) find that the financial sector attracted higher-quality workers in the 1930s and since the 1980s but not in the period when Depression-era banking regulations were in place. Before 1990 the wages of highly educated (postgraduate degree) workers in finance and engineering largely tracked one another; since 1990 wages for highly educated workers in the financial sector have grown much more rapidly than wages of highly educated engineers.

The fact that many of the most talented people are being pulled into finance is worrisome in itself. Luigi Zingales is also concerned about the ability of smart, highly paid financial sector managers to create walls around their earnings. "Thanks to its resources and cleverness, [the financial sector] has increasingly been able to rig the rules to its own advantage," he notes (Zingales 2012, 49).

---

13. The rich tend to have different preferences from the average person (opera, museums, exotic butterfly collections), which their charitable causes disproportionately support. In principle, the government could offer a sliding scale for the deductibility for such gifts, but doing so could be difficult to achieve in practice.

Table 10.1 Sources of wealth of self-made financial-sector billionaires in advanced countries and emerging economies, 2001 and 2014 (percent)

Source of wealth	2001		2014	
	Share of billionaires	Share of billionaire wealth	Share of billionaires	Share of billionaire wealth
Advanced countries				
Hedge fund	14.9	11.3	29.5	32.7
Private equity/leveraged buyout	7.5	6.7	1.1	2.3
Finance, banking, and insurance	40.3	50.2	19.5	14.6
Venture capital	4.5	1.9	2.6	1.7
Real estate	29.8	28.3	30.5	27.5
Investment and other diversified wealth	3.0	1.6	16.3	21.2
Emerging economies				
Hedge fund	4.2	5.6	0.6	0.2
Private equity/leveraged buyout	0	0	0	0
Finance, banking, and insurance	50.0	33.9	25.0	28.5
Venture capital	0	0	0	0
Real estate	29.2	42.4	48.8	39.0
Investment and other diversified wealth	16.6	18.1	25.6	32.3

Source: Author's calculations using data from Forbes, The World's Billionaires.

Dividing financial sector wealth into hedge funds; private equity; venture capital; finance, banking, and insurance; real estate; and investments and other diversified wealth highlights these concerns. Table 10.1 shows the distribution of self-made financial sector billionaires by industry in 2001 and 2014, in the North and South.

In the South, where the share of self-made financial sector wealth declined between 2001 and 2014, the largest share of financial sector billionaires' wealth (39 percent) is now from real estate. The North shows a more diversified picture, with a sharp increase in the importance of hedge funds and finance at the expense of private equity and venture capital.

The rise in real estate wealth in emerging markets may be indicative of a need for higher real estate taxes, land reform, or more transparent regulation.[14] One aim of policy should be to discourage excessive risk taking

---

14. The real estate sector has been intricately linked with financial sector problems in both advanced countries and emerging markets. Real estate speculation is a common source of

and ensure transparency in real estate transactions. In the North the rise in hedge fund wealth and the stable fortunes of real estate billionaires following the worst financial crisis since the Great Depression suggests that government policies did not equitably distribute the costs of the crisis to the sector. Following the Asian financial crisis, extreme wealth in the financial sector plummeted; to this day its share remains well below averages in 1996. The fact that the sector's wealth has grown in the United States since the crisis supports the call for reform of the financial regulatory system.

Takeaways

Many of the superrich help economies grow, create jobs, and spur development. They are often the people who make industrial and technological leaps possible. Ensuring that innovators continue to thrive is good for global growth. In the South the most important policies that can help them do so are establishment of property rights, free entry and exit of firms, and openness to trade and FDI. Ensuring that producers compete in contestable markets is critical.

There is some evidence that industrial policies that assist successful private sector exporters may help countries foster the national champions that promote growth. These policies are distinct from state capitalism (where the state is a direct player in the economy) or industrial policy that focuses on sectoral development. These kinds of policies seek to promote large-scale entrepreneurship by helping resources flow more rapidly to the most productive firms to promote modernization.

Policy can also help contain less productive sources of wealth. In some countries extreme wealth has been concentrated among heirs or in the financial sector. Limiting inheritance and financial sector wealth are best done via estate taxes and financial activity taxes.

---

costly bubbles. Concerns about real estate also include the nature of real estate transactions in some countries, such as China, where current ownership (or long-term leasing) requires government licenses and is thus susceptible to political rents.

References

Accenture. 2008. *Multi-Polar World 2: The Rise of the Emerging-Market Multinational*. Available at www.criticaleye.net/insights-servfile.cfm?id=351.

Acemoglu, Daron, Simon Johnson, and James Robinson. 2005. The Rise of Europe: Atlantic Trade, Institutional Change, and Economic Growth. *American Economic Review* 95, no. 3: 546–79.

Adams, Renée, Heitor Almeida, and Daniel Ferreira. 2005. Powerful CEOs and Their Impact on Corporate Performances. *Review of Financial Studies* 18, no. 4: 1403–32.

Ahn, Choong-Yong. 2010. Chaebol-Powered Industrial Transformation. In *Korea: From Rags to Riches*. Seoul: Korea Institute of Public Administration and Korea Times.

Aitken, Brian, Gordon Hanson, and Anne Harrison. 1997. Spillovers, Foreign Investment, and Export Behavior. *Journal of International Economics* 43, no. 1–2: 103–32.

Alvaredo, Facundo, Anthony Atkinson, Thomas Piketty, and Emmanuel Saez. 2013a. The Top 1 Percent in International and Historical Perspective. *Journal of Economic Perspectives* 27, no. 3: 3–20.

Alvaredo, Facundo, Anthony B. Atkinson, Thomas Piketty, and Emmanuel Saez. 2013b. The World Top Incomes Database. Available at http://topincomes.g-mond.parisschoolofeconomics.eu/. Accessed October 2013.

Bagchi, Sutirtha, and Jan Svejnar. 2013. *Does Wealth Inequality Matter for Growth? The Effect of Billionaire Wealth, Income Distribution, and Poverty*. IZA Discussion Paper 7733. Bonn: Institute for the Study of Labor.

Bai, Chong-En, Chang-Tai Hsieh, and Zheng Song. 2014. *Crony Capitalism with Chinese Characteristics*. Booth School of Business, University of Chicago.

Bakija, Jon, Adam Cole, and Bradley Heim. 2012. *Jobs and Income Growth of Top Earners and Causes of Changing Income Inequality: Evidence from US Tax Return Data*. Economics Department Working Paper 2010-22. Williamstown, MA: Williams College.

Banister, Judith. 2013. China's Manufacturing Employment and Hourly Labor Compensation, 2002–2009. In *International Labor Comparisons*. Washington: Bureau of Labor Statistics.

Barbero, María Inés. 1997. Argentina: Industrial Growth and Enterprise Organization, 1880–1980. In *Big Business and the Wealth of Nations*, ed. Alfred Chandler, Franco Amatori, and Takashi Hikino. Cambridge: Cambridge University Press.

Bartelsman, Eric, and Mark Doms. 2000. *Understanding Productivity: Lessons from Longitudinal Microdata*. Federal Reserve Board Working Paper 2000-19. Washington: Federal Reserve Board.

Bartelsman, Eric, John Haltiwanger, and Stefano Scarpetta. 2013. Cross-Country Differences in Productivity: The Role of Allocation and Selection. *American Economic Review* 103, no. 1: 305–34.

Baumol, William. 1990. Entrepreneurship: Productive, Unproductive, and Destructive. *Journal of Political Economy* 98, no. 5: 893–921.

Becker, Sascha, and Hans Hvide. 2013. *Do Entrepreneurs Matter?* Center for Economic Studies and IFO Institute Working Paper 4088. Munich: CESifo Group.

Bennedsen, Morten, Francisco Pérez-González, and Daniel Wolfenzon. 2007. *Do CEOs Matter?* NYU Working Paper FIN-06-032. New York: Stern School of Business, New York University.

Bento, Pedro, and Diego Restuccia. 2014. *Misallocation, Establishment Size and Productivity*. University of Toronto Working Paper Series 517.

Bernard, Andrew B., J. Bradford Jensen, and Peter K. Schott. 2009. Importers, Exporters, and Multinationals: A Portrait of U.S. Firms that Trade Goods. In *Producer Dynamics: New Evidence from Micro Data*, ed. Timothy Dunne, J. Bradford Jensen, and Mark J. Roberts. Chicago: University of Chicago Press.

Bertrand, Marianne, Simon Johnson, Krislert Samphantharak, and Antoinette Schoar. 2008. Mixing Family with Business: A Study of Thai Business Groups and the Families Behind Them. *Journal of Financial Economics* 88, no. 3: 466–98.

Bertrand, Marianne, and Antoinette Schoar. 2003. Managing with Style: The Effect of Managers on Firm Policies. *Quarterly Journal of Economics* 118, no. 4: 1169–208.

Bhagwati, Jagdish. 1982. Directly Unproductive, Profit-Seeking (DUP) Activities. *Journal of Political Economy* 90, no. 5: 988–1002.

Bhalla, Surjit. 2002. *Imagine There's No Country: Poverty, Inequality, and Growth in the Era of Globalization*. Washington: Institute for International Economics.

Bhalla, Surjit. 2012. *Devaluing to Prosperity: Misaligned Currencies and Their Growth Consequences*. Washington: Peterson Institute for International Economics.

Blalock, Garrick, and Paul Gertler. 2008. Welfare Gains from Foreign Direct Investment through Technology Transfer to Local Suppliers. *Journal of International Economics* 74, no. 2: 402–21.

BLS (Bureau of Labor Statistics). 2015. National Business Employment Dynamics Data by Firm Size. In *Business Employment Dynamics*. Washington: Bureau of Labor Statistics.

Bruce, Donald, and Mohammed Moshin. 2006. Tax Policy and Entrepreneurship: New Time Series Evidence. *Small Business Economics* 26, no. 5: 409–25. Available at http://web.utk.edu/~dbruce/sbe06.pdf.

Brush, Candida, Nancy Carter, Elizabeth Gatewood, Patricia Greene, and Myra Hart. 2004. *Gatekeepers of Venture Growth: The Role and Participation of Women in the Venture Capital Industry*. The Diana Project, Babson College, Boston.

Carnegie, Andrew. 1891. The Advantages of Poverty. In *The Gospel of Wealth and Other Timely Essays*, Edward C. Kirkland, ed. Cambridge, MA: The Belknap Press of Harvard University Press, 1962.

Carnegie Library of Pittsburgh, with the Center for Economic Development, Carnegie Mellon University. 2005. *Economic Impact Study: Regional Benefits of Carnegie Library of Pittsburgh*. Available at www.clpgh.org/about/economicimpact.

Cernat, Lucian, Ana Norman-López, and Ana Duch T-Figueras. 2014. SMEs Are More Important than You Think! Challenges and Opportunities for EU Exporting SMEs. Chief Economist Note 3, European Commission, September. Available at http://trade.ec.europa.eu/doclib/docs/2014/september/tradoc_152792.pdf.

Chandler, Alfred D. 1992. Organizational Capabilities and the Economic History of the Industrial Enterprise. *Journal of Economic Perspectives* 6, no. 3: 79–100.

Chandler, Alfred D., Jr., Franco Amatori, and Takashi Hikino, eds. 1997. *Big Business and the Wealth of Nations*. Cambridge: Cambridge University Press.

Chang, Leslie. 2009. *Factory Girls: From Village to City in a Changing China*. New York: Random House.

Chang, Roberto, Linda Kaltani, and Norman Loayza. 2009. Openness Can Be Good for Growth: The Role of Policy Complementarities. *Journal of Development Economics* 90, no. 1: 33–49.

Choudhury, Prithwiraj, and Tarun Khanna. 2013. *Do Leaders Matter? Natural Experiment and Quantitative Case Study of Indian State Owned Laboratories*. Harvard Business School Working Paper 14-077. Boston: Harvard Business School.

Claessens, Stijn, Simeon Djankov, and Larry Lang. 2000. The Separation of Ownership and Control in East Asian Corporations. *Journal of Financial Economics* 1–2: 81–112.

Clift, Jeremy. 2003. Hearing the Dogs Bark—Jeremy Clift interviews development guru Hernando de Soto. People in Economics. *Finance and Development* (December). Available at www.imf.org/external/pubs/ft/fandd/2003/12/pdf/people.pdf.

de Soto, Hernando. 1989. *The Other Path: The Invisible Revolution in the Third World*. New York: Harper Collins.

Didier, Tatiana, Ross Levine, and Sergio Schmukler. 2014. *Capital Market Financing, Firm Growth, and Firm Size Distribution*. NBER Working Paper 20336. Cambridge, MA: National Bureau of Economic Research.

Diwan, Ishac, Philip Keefer, and Marc Schiffbauer. 2014. *Private Sector Growth and Cronyism in Egypt*. Washington: World Bank.

Djankov, Simeon, Rafael La Porta, Florencio Lopez-de-Silanes, and Andrei Shleifer. 2002. The Regulation of Entry. *Quarterly Journal of Economics* 117, no. 1: 1–37.

Djankov, Simeon, Caralee McLiesh, and Andrei Shleifer. 2007. Private Credit in 129 Countries. *Journal of Financial Economics* 84, no. 2: 299–329.

Dobbs, Richard, Jaana Remes, Sven Smit, James Manyika, Jonathan Woetzel, and Yaw Agyenim-Boateng. 2013. *Urban world: The shifting global business landscape*. McKinsey Global Institute (October).

Doti, Frank J. 2003. Estate Tax Repeal: Historical Data Indicate Philanthropy May Suffer. *Tax Notes* 99.

Edwards, Lawrence, and Robert Z. Lawrence. 2013. *Rising Tide: Is Growth in Emerging Economies Good for the United States?* Washington: Peterson Institute for International Economics.

European Commission. 2015. Annual Enterprise Statistics by Size Class for Special Aggregates of Activities (NACE Rev. 2). *Eurostat.* Available at http://ec.europa.eu/eurostat/web/structural-business-statistics/data/database.

Fernandes, Ana, Caroline Freund, and M. Denisse Pierola. 2015. Exporter Behavior, Country Size and Stage of Development. *Journal of Development Economics,* forthcoming.

Fogel, Kathy, Randall Morck, and Bernard Young. 2008. Big Business Stability and Economic Growth: Is What's Good for General Motors Good for America? *Journal of Financial Economics* 89, no. 1: 83–108.

Folsom, Burton. 1987. *The Myth of the Robber Barons: A New Look at the Rise of Big Business in America.* Hemdon, VA: Young America's Foundation.

Foster, Lucia, John Haltiwanger, and C. J. Krizan. 2001. Aggregate Productivity Growth: Lessons from Microeconomic Evidence. In *New Developments in Productivity Analysis,* ed. Charles Hulten, Edwin Dean, and Michael Harper. Chicago: University of Chicago Press.

Freeland, Chrystia. 2012. *Plutocrats: The Rise of the New Global Super-Rich and the Fall of Everyone Else.* New York: Penguin.

Freund, Caroline, and Bineswaree Bolaky. 2008. Trade, Regulations, and Income. *Journal of Development Economics* 87, no. 2: 309–21.

Freund, Caroline, and Sarah Oliver. 2016. *The Origins of the Superrich: The Billionaire Characteristics Database.* PIIE Working Paper 16-1. Washington: Peterson Institute for International Economics.

Freund, Caroline, and M. Denisse Pierola. 2012. Export Surges. *Journal of Development Economics* 97, no. 2: 387–95.

Freund, Caroline, and M. Denisse Pierola. 2015. Export Superstars. *Review of Economics and Statistics* 97, no. 5 (December): 1023–32.

Gabaix, Xavier, and Augustin Landier. 2008. Why Has CEO Pay Increased So Much? *Quarterly Journal of Economics* 121, no. 1: 49–100.

Gandhi, Aditi, and Michael Walton. 2012. Where Do Indian Billionaires Get Their Wealth? *Economic and Political Weekly* 47, no. 40: 10–14.

García-Santana, Manuel, and Josep Pijoan-Mas. 2014. The Reservation Laws in India and the Misallocation of Production Factors. *Journal of Monetary Economics* 66: 193–209.

Gompers, Paul, Vladimir Mukharlyamov, Emily Weisburst, and Yuhai Xuan. 2014. *Gender Effects in Venture Capital.* SSRN Working Paper, Social Science Research Network.

Grisham, John. 1999. *The Testament.* New York: Doubleday.

Guillén, Mauro, and Esteban García-Canal. 2013. *Emerging Markets Rule: Growth Strategies of the New Global Giants.* New York: McGraw-Hill.

Haltiwanger, John, Ron Jarmin, and Javier Miranda. 2013. Who Creates Jobs? Small vs. Large vs. Young. *Review of Economics and Statistics* 45, no. 2: 347–61.

Haskel, Jonathan, Robert Z. Lawrence, Edward E. Leamer, and Matthew J. Slaughter. 2012. Globalization and U.S. Wages: Modifying Classic Theory to Explain Recent Facts. *Journal of Economic Perspectives* 26, no. 2: 119–40.

Hausmann, Ricardo, Lant Pritchett, and Dani Rodrik. 2005. Growth Accelerations. *Journal of Economic Growth* 10, no. 4: 303–29.

Holtz-Eakin, Douglas, David Joulfaian, and Harvey S. Rosen. 1993. The Carnegie Conjecture: Some Empirical Evidence. *Quarterly Journal of Economics* 108, no. 2 (May): 413–35.

Hsieh, Chang-Tai, and Peter Klenow. 2009. Misallocation and Manufacturing TFP in China and India. *Quarterly Journal of Economics* 124, no. 4: 1403–48.

Hsieh, Chang-Tai, and Peter Klenow. 2014. The Life Cycle of Plants in India and Mexico. *Quarterly Journal of Economics* 129, no. 3: 1035–84.

Hsieh, Chang-Tai, and Benjamin A. Olken. 2014. The Missing Middle. *Journal of Economic Perspectives* 28, no. 3: 89–108.

Huber, Evelyne, Dietrich Rueschemeyer, and John D. Stephens. 1993. The Impact of Economic Development on Democracy. *Journal of Economic Perspectives* 7, no. 3: 71–86.

Ibarraran, Pablo, Alessandro Maffioli, and Rodolfo Stucchi. 2009. *SME Policy and Firms' Productivity in Latin America*. IZA Discussion Paper 4486. Bonn: Institute for Labor.

IFC (International Finance Corporation). 2013. *Assessing Private Sector Contributions to Job Creation and Poverty Reduction*. Washington.

Jantti, M., E. Sierminska, and T. Smeeding. 2008. *The Joint Distribution of Household Income and Wealth: Evidence from the Luxembourg Wealth Study*. OECD Social, Employment and Migration Working Paper 65. Paris: OECD Publishing.

Javorcik, Beata. 2004. Does Foreign Direct Investment Increase the Productivity of Domestic Firms? In Search of Spillovers through Backward Linkages. *American Economic Review* 94, no. 3: 605–27.

Jha, Saumitra. 2015. Financial Asset Holdings and Political Attitudes: Evidence from Revolutionary England. *Quarterly Journal of Economics* 103, no. 3.

Jones, Benjamin, and Ben Olken. 2008. The Anatomy of Start-Stop Growth. *Review of Economics and Statistics* 90, no. 3: 582–87.

Josephson, Matthew. 1934. *The Robber Barons: The Great American Capitalists, 1861–1901*. New York: Harcourt, Brace and Company.

Kampfner, John. 2014. *The Rich: From Slaves to Super-Yachts: A 2,000-Year History*. London: Little Brown.

Kaplan, Steven, and Joshua Rauh. 2013. It's the Market: The Broad-Based Rise in the Return to Top Talent. *Journal of Economic Perspectives* 27, no. 3: 35–56. Available at http://hdl.handle.net/10419/63536.

Khanna, Tarun, Jaeyong Song, and Kyungmook Lee. 2011. The Paradox of Samsung's Rise. *Harvard Business Review* 89, nos. 7–8 (July–August): 142–47.

Knight Frank. 2014. *The Wealth Report*. London.

Kopczuk, Wojciech. 2007. Bequest and Tax Planning: Evidence from Estate Tax Returns. *Quarterly Journal of Economics* 122, no. 4: 1801–54.

Kopczuk, Wojciech. 2015. What Do We Know about the Evolution of Top Wealth Shares in the United States? *Journal of Economic Perspectives* 29, no. 1: 47–66

Kotschwar, Barbara, and Tyler Moran. 2015. Balancing the Board: A Global Survey of Women in Corporate Leadership. Unpublished paper. Peterson Institute for International Economics, Washington.

Krueger, Anne. 1974. The Political Economy of the Rent-Seeking Society. *American Economic Review* 64, no. 3: 291–303.

Lakner, Cristoph, and Branko Milanović. 2013. *Global Income Distribution: From the Fall of the Berlin Wall to the Great Recession.* World Bank Policy Research Working Paper 6719. Washington: World Bank.

La Porta, Rafael, Florencio Lopez-de-Silanes, Andrei Shleifer, and Robert Vishny. 1997. Legal Determinants of External Finance. *Journal of Finance* 52, no. 3: 1131–50.

Lardy, Nicholas. 2014. *Markets over Mao: The Rise of Private Business in China.* Washington: Peterson Institute for International Economics.

Lipset, Seymour. 1959. Some Social Requisites of Democracy: Economic Development and Political Legitimacy. *American Political Science Review* 53, no. 1: 69–105.

Lizzeri, Alessandro, and Nicola Persico. 2004. Why Did the Elites Extend the Suffrage? Democracy and the Scope of Government, with an Application to Britain's "Age of Reform." *Quarterly Journal of Economics* 119, no. 2: 707–65.

Lundberg, Ferdinand.1968. *The Rich and the Super-Rich.* Secaucus, NJ: Lyle Stuart.

Markle, Kevin, and Douglas Shackelford. 2012. Cross-Country Comparisons of Corporate Income Taxes. *National Tax Journal* 65, no. 3 (September): 493–528.

Mariniello, Mario. 2013. *The Dragon Awakes: Is Chinese Competition Policy a Cause for Concern?* Policy Contribution (October 22). Brussels: Bruegel.

Marshall, Alfred. 1890. *Principles of Economics.* London: Macmillan and Co., Ltd.

Martin, Leslie, Shanthi Nataraj, and Ann Harrison. 2014. *In with the Big, Out with the Small: Removing Small-Scale Reservations in India.* NBER Working Paper 19942. Cambridge, MA: National Bureau of Economic Research.

McMillan, Margaret, Dani Rodrik, and Inigo Verduzco-Gallo. 2014. Globalization, Structural Change and Development. *World Development* 63: 11–32.

Milanović, Branko. 2005. *Worlds Apart: Measuring International and Global Inequality.* Princeton, NJ: Princeton University Press.

Milanović, Branko. 2014. *All the Ginis Dataset.* Washington: World Bank.

Moran, Theodore. 2011. *Foreign Direct Investment and Development.* Washington: Peterson Institute for International Economics.

Morikawa, Hidemasa. 1997. Japan: Increasing Organizational Capabilities of Large Industrial Enterprises, 1880s–1980s. In *Big Business and the Wealth of Nations,* ed. Alfred D. Chandler, Jr., Franco Amatori, and Takashi Hikino. Cambridge: Cambridge University Press.

Murphy, Kevin, Andrei Shleifer, and Robert Vishny. 1991. The Allocation of Talent: Implications for Growth. *Quarterly Journal of Economics* 106, no. 2: 503–30.

Park, Chung-hee. 1962. *Our Nation's Path: Ideology for Social Reconstruction.* Seoul: Dong-a Publishing Company.

Pempel, T. J. 1998. *Regime Shift: Comparative Dynamics of the Japanese Political Economy.* Ithaca, NY: Cornell University Press.

Philippon, Thomas, and Ariell Reshef. 2009. *Wages and Human Capital in the U.S. Financial Industry: 1909–2006.* NBER Working Paper 14644. Cambridge, MA: National Bureau of Economic Research.

Philippon, Thomas, and Ariell Reshef. 2013. An International Look at the Growth of Modern Finance. *Journal of Economic Perspectives* 27, no. 2: 73–96.

Phillips, Kevin. 2002. *Wealth and Democracy: A Political History of the American Rich.* New York: Broadway Books.

Piketty, Thomas. 2014. *Capital in the Twenty-First Century.* Cambridge, MA: Belknap Press.

Piketty, Thomas, and Emmanuel Saez. 2013. A Theory of Optimal Inheritance Taxation. *Econometrica* 81, no. 5: 1851–86.

Quigley, Timothy, and Donald Hambrick. 2012. When the Former CEO Stayed on as Board Chair: Effects on Successor Discretion, Strategic Change and Performance. *Strategic Management Journal* 33, no. 7: 834–59.

Ravallion, Martin. 2012. Why Don't We See Poverty Convergence? *American Economic Review* 102, no. 1: 504–23.

Rijkers, Bob, Hassen Arrouri, Caroline Freund, and Antonio Nucifora. 2014. Which Firms Create the Most Jobs in Developing Countries? Evidence from Tunisia. *Labour Economics* 31: 84–102.

Rijkers, Bob, Caroline Freund, and Antonio Nucifora. 2014. *All in the Family: State Capture in Tunisia.* World Bank Policy Research Working Paper 6810 (March). Washington: World Bank.

Robinson, Robert V., and Carl M. Briggs. 1991. The Rise of Nineteenth Century Indianapolis. *American Journal of Sociology* 97, no. 3: 622–56.

Rodrik, Dani. 2015. Premature Deindustrialization. Photocopy. Harvard University.

Rosen, Sherwin. 1981. The Economics of Superstars. *American Economic Review* 71, no. 5: 845–58.

Schröter, Harm G. 1997. European Enterprise: Strategies of Adaptation and Renewal in the Twentieth Century. *Business History Review* 71, no. 4: 636–37.

Seery, Emma, and Ana Caistor Arendar. 2014. *Even It Up: Time to End Extreme Inequality* Oxford: Oxfam. Available at www.oxfam.org/sites/www.oxfam.org/files/file_attachments/cr-even-it-up-extreme-inequality-291014-en.pdf.

Spero, Joan. 2014. *Charity and Philanthropy in Russia, China, India and Brazil.* New York: Foundation Center.

Subramanian, Arvind. 2011. *Eclipse: Living in the Shadow of China's Economic Dominance.* Washington: Peterson Institute for International Economics.

Syverson, Chad. 2004. Product Substitutability and Productivity Dispersion. *Review of Economics and Statistics* 86, no. 2: 534–50.

van Agtmael, Antoine. 2007. *The Emerging Markets Century: How a New Breed of World Class Companies Is Overtaking the World.* New York: Free Press.

van Ark, Bart, Abdul Azeez Erumban, Vivian Chen, and Ustav Kumar. 2010. The Cost Competitiveness of Manufacturing in China and India: An Industry and Regional Perspective. In *Emerging Giants: China and India in the World Economy,* ed. Barry Eichengreen, Poonam Gupta, and Rajiv Kumar. Oxford: Oxford University Press.

Van Biesebroeck, Johannes. 2005. Firm Size Matters: Growth and Productivity Growth in African Manufacturing. *Economic Development and Cultural Change* 53, no. 3: 545–84.

Verme, Paolo, Branko Milanović, Sherine Al-Shawarby, Sahar El Tawila, May Gadallah, and Enas Ali A. El-Majeed. 2014. *Inside Inequality in the Arab Republic of Egypt*. Washington: World Bank. Available at www.worldbank.org/content/dam/Worldbank/egypt-inequality-book.pdf.

Véron, Nicolas. 2008. *The Demographics of Corporate Champions*. Bruegel Working Paper 2008-03. Brussels: Bruegel.

Wealth-X and UBS. 2014. *World Ultra Wealth Report*. Singapore.

Wegenroth, Ulrich. 1997. Germany: Competition Abroad, Cooperation at Home, 1870–1990. In *Big Business and the Wealth of Nations*, ed. Alfred D. Chandler, Jr., Franco Amatori, and Takashi Hikino. Cambridge: Cambridge University Press.

West, Darrell. 2014. *Billionaires: Reflections on the Upper Crust*. Washington: Brookings Institution.

West, Max. 1980. *The Inheritance Tax*. New York: Columbia University Press.

Wolff, Edward. 2010. *Recent Trends in Household Wealth in the United States: Rising Debt and the Middle-Class Squeeze—An Update to 2007*. Levy Economics Institute Working Paper 589. Annandale-on-Hudson, New York: Bard College.

World Bank. 2012. *World Development Report on Gender Equality and Development*. Washington.

World Bank. 2014. *Gender at Work*. Washington: World Bank, Gender and Development Unit. Available at www.worldbank.org/content/dam/Worldbank/document/Gender/GenderAtWork_web.pdf.

Yudanov, Andrei. 1997. Large Enterprises in the USSR: The Functional Disorder. In *Big Business and the Wealth of Nations*, ed. Alfred D. Chandler, Jr., Franco Amatori, and Takashi Hikino. Cambridge: Cambridge University Press.

Zakaria, Fareed. 2011. *The Post-American World: Release 2.0*. New York: W. W. Norton & Company.

Zingales, Luigi. 2012. *A Capitalism for the People: Recapturing the Lost Genius of American Prosperity*. New York: Basic Books, Perseus.

Index

Anheuser-Busch, 53, 72
Apple, 62, 105, 105t, 106f
Arab Spring, 156–57
Arango, Jeronimo, 87
Arcelik, 2
Argentina, 79
Arnall, Sue Ann, 25
Asia. *See also specific country*
    crony capitalism in, 77–78, 81
    globalized firms in, 108
    size of firms in, 75–79
    sources of wealth in, 31, 35–36, 45
    superrich in, 34, 34t, 35f, 35–36, 37t–41t, 45
Association of Southeast Asian Nations (ASEAN), 36
Aventis (Hoechst), 69

Baidu, 35, 63, 94, 108
Bangladesh, 88
BASF, 69, 70
Bayer, 69, 70
Bayer, Friedrich, 70
Ben Ali, 80–81
Benetton, Giuliana, 125
Benz, Karl, 70
Bermuda, 173
Bestseller, 75
Botelho, Mauricio, 171
Bettencourt, Liliane, 18, 118
Bharat Forge, 50–51
big firms. *See* mega firms
billionaire class. *See* superrich
Birkeland, Kristian, 75
Blakely, Sara, 120, 125
Blavatnik, Leonard, 177
Bombardier, 171
Bozano, Julio, 171
Brazil
    despachante, 165
    development in, 71f, 71–72
    employees per firm in, 87, 88f
    industrial policy in, 170–71
    mega firms in, 65, 66f, 67
    philanthropy in, 177
    regulation in, 165
    sources of wealth in, 41, 42t
BRF, 87
BRICS countries. *See also specific country*

development in, 71f, 71–72
employees per firm in, 87, 88f
mega firms in, 65, 66f, 67
philanthropy in, 177
sources of wealth in, 41–43, 42t
Brito, Carlos, 96
Buffett, Warren, 62, 145
Burch, Tory, 125
bureaucracy, 164–65
business climate, 9, 163–72
business networks, 123–24
Byanyima, Winnie, 15

Cadogan Estates, 131n
Calderon Rojas, Francisco, 87
Calderon Rojas, Jose, 87
California Packing (Del Monte), 72
Campbell Soup, 73
capital
    allocation of (*See* resource allocation)
    returns to, 100–101
capitalism, 86
capital markets, development of, 171–72
Caraco Pharma, 101
Carlsberg, 74
Carnegie, Andrew, 72, 173, 176, 178
Carrefour, 80
Carter, Amon, 176
Casino, 80
Celtel, 44
Cencosud, 80, 87
CEOs, 62–65
Cevital, 44
chaebol, 76, 86, 168
Chandler, Alfred, 6
Chang, Leslie, 88
Chang Yun Chung, 77
Chan Laiwa, 118
Chapman, James, 176
Chaudhary, Binod, 45
Cheezheng Tibetan Medicine, 117
Chen, Leo, 127
Chery, 78–79
Cheung Yan, 35
Chile, 80, 102–103
China
    banking sector in, 94
    competition policy in, 83
    crony capitalism in, 77–78

Other Publications from the Peterson Institute for International Economics

POLICY BRIEFS

* = out of print

POLICY ANALYSES IN INTERNATIONAL ECONOMICS Series

China's Rise: Challenges and Opportunities
C. Fred Bergsten, Charles Freeman, Nicholas R. Lardy, and Derek J. Mitchell
September 2008   ISBN 978-0-88132-417-4

Banking on Basel: The Future of International Financial Regulation   Daniel K. Tarullo
September 2008   ISBN 978-0-88132-423-5

US Pension Reform: Lessons from Other Countries   Martin Neil Baily and Jacob Funk Kirkegaard
February 2009   ISBN 978-0-88132-425-9

How Ukraine Became a Market Economy and Democracy   Anders Åslund
March 2009   ISBN 978-0-88132-427-3

Global Warming and the World Trading System
Gary Clyde Hufbauer, Steve Charnovitz, and Jisun Kim
March 2009   ISBN 978-0-88132-428-0

The Russia Balance Sheet   Anders Åslund and Andrew Kuchins
March 2009   ISBN 978-0-88132-424-2

The Euro at Ten: The Next Global Currency?
Jean Pisani-Ferry and Adam S. Posen, eds.
July 2009   ISBN 978-0-88132-430-3

Financial Globalization, Economic Growth, and the Crisis of 2007–09   William R. Cline
May 2010   ISBN 978-0-88132-4990-0

Russia after the Global Economic Crisis
Anders Åslund, Sergei Guriev, and Andrew Kuchins, eds.
June 2010   ISBN 978-0-88132-497-6

Sovereign Wealth Funds: Threat or Salvation?
Edwin M. Truman
September 2010   ISBN 978-0-88132-498-3

The Last Shall Be the First: The East European Financial Crisis, 2008–10   Anders Åslund
October 2010   ISBN 978-0-88132-521-8

Witness to Transformation: Refugee Insights into North Korea   Stephan Haggard and Marcus Noland
January 2011   ISBN 978-0-88132-438-9

Foreign Direct Investment and Development: Launching a Second Generation of Policy Research, Avoiding the Mistakes of the First, Reevaluating Policies for Developed and Developing Countries   Theodore H. Moran
April 2011   ISBN 978-0-88132-600-0

How Latvia Came through the Financial Crisis
Anders Åslund and Valdis Dombrovskis
May 2011   ISBN 978-0-88132-602-4

Global Trade in Services: Fear, Facts, and Offshoring   J. Bradford Jensen
August 2011   ISBN 978-0-88132-601-7

NAFTA and Climate Change   Meera Fickling and Jeffrey J. Schott
September 2011   ISBN 978-0-88132-436-5

Eclipse: Living in the Shadow of China's Economic Dominance   Arvind Subramanian
September 2011   ISBN 978-0-88132-606-2

Flexible Exchange Rates for a Stable World Economy   Joseph E. Gagnon with Marc Hinterschweiger
September 2011 I   SBN 978-0-88132-627-7

The Arab Economies in a Changing World, 2d ed.   Marcus Noland and Howard Pack
November 2011   ISBN 978-0-88132-628-4

Sustaining China's Economic Growth After the Global Financial Crisis   Nicholas R. Lardy
January 2012   ISBN 978-0-88132-626-0

Who Needs to Open the Capital Account?
Olivier Jeanne, Arvind Subramanian, and John Williamson
April 2012   ISBN 978-0-88132-511-9

Devaluing to Prosperity: Misaligned Currencies and Their Growth Consequences   Surjit S. Bhalla
August 2012   ISBN 978-0-88132-623-9

Private Rights and Public Problems: The Global Economics of Intellectual Property in the 21st Century   Keith E. Maskus
September 2012   ISBN 978-0-88132-507-2

Global Economics in Extraordinary Times: Essays in Honor of John Williamson
C. Fred Bergsten and C. Randall Henning, eds.
November 2012   ISBN 978-0-88132-662-8

Rising Tide: Is Growth in Emerging Economies Good for the United States?   Lawrence Edwards and Robert Z. Lawrence
February 2013   ISBN 978-0-88132-500-3

Responding to Financial Crisis: Lessons from Asia Then, the United States and Europe Now
Changyong Rhee and Adam S. Posen, eds
October 2013   ISBN 978-0-88132-674-1

Fueling Up: The Economic Implications of America's Oil and Gas Boom   Trevor Houser and Shashank Mohan
January 2014   ISBN 978-0-88132-656-7

How Latin America Weathered the Global Financial Crisis   José De Gregorio
January 2014   ISBN 978-0-88132-678-9

Confronting the Curse: The Economics and Geopolitics of Natural Resource Governance
Cullen S. Hendrix and Marcus Noland
May 2014   ISBN 978-0-88132-676-5

Inside the Euro Crisis: An Eyewitness Account
Simeon Djankov
June 2014   ISBN 978-0-88132-685-7

Managing the Euro Area Debt Crisis
William R. Cline
June 2014   ISBN 978-0-88132-678-1

Markets over Mao: The Rise of Private Business in China   Nicholas R. Lardy
September 2014   ISBN 978-0-88132-693-2

Bridging the Pacific: Toward Free Trade and Investment between China and the United States
C. Fred Bergsten, Gary Clyde Hufbauer, and Sean Miner. Assisted by Tyler Moran
October 2014   ISBN 978-0-88132-691-8

The Great Rebirth: Lessons from the Victory of Capitalism over Communism
Anders Åslund and Simeon Djankov, eds.
November 2014   ISBN 978-0-88132-697-0

Ukraine: What Went Wrong and How to Fix It
Anders Åslund
April 2015   ISBN 978-0-88132-701-4

From Stress to Growth: Strengthening Asia's Financial Systems in a Post-Crisis World
Marcus Noland; Donghyun Park, eds.
October 2015   ISBN 978-0-88132-699-4

The Great Tradeoff: Confronting Moral
Conflicts in the Era of Globalization
Steven R. Weisman
January 2016   ISBN 978-0-88132-695-6
Rich People, Poor Countries: The Rise of
Emerging-Market Tycoons and their Mega
Firms   Caroline Freund, assisted by Sarah Oliver
January 2016   ISBN 978-0-88132-703-8

SPECIAL REPORTS

1   Promoting World Recovery: A Statement on
      Global Economic Strategy*   by Twenty-six
      Economists from Fourteen Countries
      December 1982   ISBN 0-88132-013-7
2   Prospects for Adjustment in Argentina,
      Brazil, and Mexico: Responding to the Debt
      Crisis*   John Williamson, ed.
      June 1983   ISBN 0-88132-016-1
3   Inflation and Indexation: Argentina, Brazil,
      and Israel*   John Williamson, ed.
      March 1985   ISBN 0-88132-037-4
4   Global Economic Imb alances*
      C. Fred Bergsten, ed.
      March 1986   ISBN 0-88132-042-0
5   African Debt and Financing*Carol Lancaster
      and John Williamson, eds.
      May 1986   ISBN 0-88132-044-7
6   Resolving the Global Economic Crisis: After
      Wall Street* by Thirty-three Economists from
      Thirteen Countries
      December 1987   ISBN 0-88132-070-6
7   World Economic Problems*
      Kimberly Ann Elliott and John Williamson, *eds.*
      April 1988   ISBN 0-88132-055-2
      Reforming World Agricultural Trade*
      by Twenty-nine Professionals from Seventeen
      Countries
      1988   ISBN 0-88132-088-9
8   Economic Relations Between the United
      States and Korea: Conflict or Cooperation?*
      Thomas O. Bayard and Soogil Young, eds.
      January 1989   ISBN 0-88132-068-4
9   Whither APEC? The Progress to Date and
      Agenda for the Future*   C. Fred Bergsten, ed.
      October 1997   ISBN 0-88132-248-2
10   Economic Integration of the Korean
      Peninsula   Marcus Noland, ed.
      January 1998   ISBN 0-88132-255-5
11   Restarting Fast Track*   Jeffrey J. Schott, ed.
      April 1998   ISBN 0-88132-259-8
12   Launching New Global Trade Talks: An
      Action Agenda   Jeffrey J. Schott, ed.
      September 1998   ISBN 0-88132-266-0
13   Japan's Financial Crisis and Its Parallels to
      US Experience   Ryoichi Mikitani and
      Adam S. Posen, eds.
      September 2000   ISBN 0-88132-289-X
14   The Ex-Im Bank in the 21st Century: A New
      Approach   Gary Clyde Hufbauer and Rita M.
      Rodriguez, eds.
      January 2001   ISBN 0-88132-300-4

15   The Korean Diaspora in the World
      Economy   C. Fred Bergsten and
      Inbom Choi, eds.
      January 2003   ISBN 0-88132-358-6
16   Dollar Overvaluation and the World
      Economy   C. Fred Bergsten and
      John Williamson, eds.
      February 2003   ISBN 0-88132-351-9
17   Dollar Adjustment: How Far? Against
      What? C. Fred Bergsten and John Williamson,
      eds.
      November 2004   ISBN 0-88132-378-0
18   The Euro at Five: Ready for a Global Role?
      Adam S. Posen, ed.
      April 2005   ISBN 0-88132-380-2
19   Reforming the IMF for the 21st Century
      Edwin M. Truman, ed.
      April 2006   ISBN 978-0-88132-387-0
20   The Long-Term International Economic
      Position of the United States
      C. Fred Bergsten, ed.
      May 2009   ISBN 978-0-88132-432-7
21   Resolving the European Debt Crisis
      William R. Cline and Guntram B. Wolff, eds.
      February 2012   ISBN 978-0-88132-642-0
22   Transatlantic Economic Challenges in an
      Era of Growing Multipolarity
      Jacob Funk Kirkegaard, Nicolas Véron, and
      Guntram B. Wolff, eds.
      June 2012   ISBN 978-0-88132-645-1

PIIE Briefings

14-1   Flirting With Default: Issues Raised by
        Debt Confrontations in the United States
        February 2014
14-2   The US-China-Europe Economic
        Reform Agenda. Papers presented at a
        Symposium in Beijing   *May 2014*
14-3   NAFTA: 20 Years Later   *November 2014*
14-4   Lessons from Decades Lost: Economic
        Challenges and Opportunities Facing
        Japan and the United States (with
        Sasakawa Peace Foundation USA)
        December 2014
14-5   Rebuilding Europe's Common Future:
        Combining Growth and Reform in the
        Euro Area   *December 2014*
15-1   Toward a US-China Investment Treaty
        February 2015   ISBN 978-0-88132-707-6
15-2   Raising Lower-Level Wages: When and
        Why It Makes Economic Sense
        April 2015   ISBN 978-0-88132-709-3
15-3   China's Economic Transformation:
        Lessons, Impact, and the Path Forward
        September 2015   ISBN 978-0-88132-709-0
15-4   India's Rise: A Strategy for Trade-Led
        Growth   C. Fred Bergsten
        September 2015   ISBN 978-0-88132-710-6

WORKS IN PROGRESS

International Monetary Cooperation: Lessons
from the Plaza Accord After Thirty Years
C. Fred Bergsten and Russell A. Green, editors

Visit our website at: www.piie.com
E-mail orders to: petersonmail@presswarehouse.com

International Sales
United Kingdom, Europe (including Russia and Turkey), Africa, and Israel

The Eurospan Group
c/o Turpin Distribution
Pegasus Drive
Stratton Business Park
Biggleswade, Bedfordshire
SG18 8TQ
United Kingdom

Tel: 44 (0) 1767-604972
Fax: 44 (0) 1767-601640

Email: eurospan@turpin-distribution.com
www.eurospangroup.com/bookstore